COACHING
the
Age
Group
Swimmer

by Lynn Hovde

Photographs by
Richard Wille

Published by
Blue Horizons Publishing Company
Quilcene, Washington

Library of Congress Catalog Card Number: 97-094379

ISBN 0-9660297-0-4

Front cover photograph by Richard Wille

Printed in the United States of America.

Blue Horizons Publishing Company
P.O. BOX 864
Quilcene, Washington 98376

In loving memory

of my father,
Raymond F. Wille,

and of my brother,
Raymond F. Wille, Jr.

Acknowledgments

I want to thank the following swimmers and coaches for modeling: Shelley Chamberlin, Scott Miller, Kagan Shopenn, and especially Nicole Hay. Also, I want to acknowledge those who were at the 1995 Age-Group Regionals at the King County Aquatic Center in Federal Way, Washington, who were photographed, but whose names are unknown. I want to thank my mother, who was an active swim-team parent in my youth and who read this book from cover to cover, offering advice, prior to it going to press; my brother Richard, who was an age-group swimmer and who took the photographs; and my husband Larry, who was supportive throughout this project. Lastly, I want to thank those coaches and pool administrators who encouraged me as a swimmer, as a WSI, and as a coach: Soupy Sales (Richmond, Virginia), Joe Rogers (Potomac, Maryland), Ray Nicoletta (Glastonbury, Connecticut), Ted Brindamour (Manchester, Connecticut), and Warren Steurer (Port Townsend, Washington).

Lynn Hovde

CONTENTS

PART ONE

Characteristics of
an Effective Coach

Membership and credentials

A swimming coach should hold the following credentials: Lifeguarding Today (which includes First Aid), CPR for the Professional Rescuer, Safety Training for Coaches, and Water Safety Instructor (WSI). A coach must be a member of USA Swimming in order for his or her team to participate in USA Swimming sanctioned swim meets. USA Swimming, based at the Olympic Training Center in Colorado Springs, is part of FINA, the international swimming organization that oversees all competitive aquatic sports.

While USA Swimming does not require coaches to be Lifeguarding Today certified, they do require anyone on deck to hold current cards in CPR, First Aid, and Safety Training for Coaches. But without Lifeguarding Today certification, a coach's options are limited. A lifeguard must be present in order for the coach to conduct practice. Hiring one coach and one lifeguard is more costly than hiring one person who is both.

If a coach has Lifeguarding Today certification, he or she must still obtain a Safety Training for Swim Coaches card; the coaching course covers similar material, but addresses additional hazards faced in a swim team practice situation. A coach needs not only safety training, but also a genuine awareness of the importance of the safety at all times for anyone in or around the pool. A coach needs to be prepared for an emergency by knowing how to prevent accidents from happening and what steps to take if an accident occurs.

Adult CPR (required by USA Swimming) teaches basic CPR skills to people in a community, whether their job requires them to provide care or not. Although USA Swimming does not require CPR for the Professional Rescuer (CPR-PR), the American Red Cross includes this in its Lifeguarding Today course. CPR-PR includes adult, child, infant, and two-man CPR, as well as bag-valve mask skills, and is specifically designed for people like lifeguards and coaches who, when on the job, have a legal responsibility to act and provide care in an emergency.

USA Swimming does not require a WSI certificate, but a coach should have prior experience as a swim instructor before coaching. It helps to know teaching principles, learned in the American Red Cross Instructor Candidate Training course, and helps to have some teaching experience with lower levels before taking on advanced students.

A coach should become a member of American Swim Coaches' Association (ASCA), which offers an endless flow of valuable information through video and audio tapes, magazines, home study courses, and clinics (around the country and worldwide). ASCA, based in Orlando, Florida, educates and certifies American swim coaches with a goal to raise both coaching and swimming

3

standards. Becoming a member of the American Swim Coaches Association is like joining a team; it's a way to network with other coaching professionals.

ASCA presents home-study courses for certification: Level 1, Foundations of Coaching; Level 2, The Stroke School; Level 3, The Physiology School; Level 4, The Administration School; and Level 5, The Leadership School.

Certification may be—to some people—just a piece of paper. But to me it is a symbol of knowledge acquired. This piece of paper requires work—study and often skill—and is proof that the owner possesses the level of education needed to perform a particular job at least adequately. Without certification, a coach may or may not have the knowledge or the skill.

Knowledge

In order to be an effective swim coach, you must know proper stroke techniques, training principles and methods, and the rules and strategies of competition. And the more you know, the better coach you are. If you feel there is a gap in your knowledge, you can reference books, magazines, video tapes, and audio tapes from a variety of swimming and coaching organizations and catalogues. The Internet is also a valuable source of information.

Research helps the experienced coach as well as the rookie, for techniques are always changing. Also, while you may know a lot, you can spend a lifetime in this sport and always learn more. You learn not by existing in a vacuum, but rather by exposing yourself to the wealth of information available. Attending clinics and talking to other coaches, sharing ideas and discussing different approaches and styles can only deepen your knowledge. Sharing what you value increases the meaning of something.

Experience

A coach needs experience as a competitive swimmer; he or she must possess swimming ability and must be able to demonstrate skills in the pool when necessary. A coach should be a swimmer still swimming, an athlete still fit; he or she should swim laps regularly. I recommend a minimum of three (one hour) workouts per week. Participating in Masters will require more than the minimum and will show swimmers you are serious about the sport. In a different practice, you work as hard as your swimmers for similar goals. Whether coaches are still competing or not, a coach who is lifeguarding needs to be able to execute a water rescue (despite the rule to reach and throw before going), which means maintaining a certain level of fitness.

Not every great or good swimmer can coach or even wants to. But every great or good coach has to have been a good swimmer in order to have the in-depth knowledge and experience to verbalize and demonstrate the skills. Some people may disagree and say there have been good coaches in various sports who aren't or haven't been athletes in that sport. They say that a coach just needs to have the eye for what is right and wrong and the ability to make corrections and bring out the best in others. I say you cannot be an effective head swimming coach unless you have experience as a swimmer, WSI, and assistant or co-coach.

A coach who doesn't swim cannot have the same connection with what he or she is teaching as a true swimmer and lover of the water does. When new techniques come along, you have to dive in the water and try them out in order to be effective in teaching others. Otherwise, you will not know what it is like to *feel* each part of a stroke, to hit some pitch with the hand and push through the water. I like the word pitch, because I often feel when I grab the water that I have a ball in my hand and I am pitching it into a certain water pocket in order to hit that perfect curve.

When coaching synchronized swimming in my late teens, I practiced various drills, trying to master the feel for the support scull. When I finally had it, I was better able to tell swimmers what to do. I remember wishing I had a coach to give me some idea of what it felt like and what I wasn't doing at the time to own that feeling. I believe that children want to succeed at a skill, and they know when they have it and when they don't. They want the coach to tell them how to do it.

"Practice makes perfect" applies to both coach and swimmer. The longer you coach, the better you get. Each season you plan the course and follow it, making adjustments along the way; and each season improves as you learn from the previous season. You can feel good about the improvements in the swimmers, in your coaching, in the team, and the way the season went; you can also evaluate what can be changed and made better the next season.

You need to do a certain amount of listening to lectures, reading, studying, thinking, and planning, but you also need to coach and learn through trial and error; your skills will grow with experience. You will make mistakes, but you have to swallow them, along with your pride, and go on to be better.

Being a role model

The coach may be a key person in a young swimmer's life. He or she can give young swimmers, who come and go from one season to the next, a positive and unforgettable experience. That is why it is important for a coach to set the proper example, to act ethically and professionally at all times.

A coach should enforce and also follow pool rules. There is nothing worse than a coach who comes to work with a bagged lunch containing a drink in a glass bottle. Before or after coaching, he sits at the poolside eating while all the swimmers, who frequent the pool, know the rules. "No eating on the deck and no glass containers in the pool area."

A coach must dress appropriately for work at a pool—in a bathing suit with shorts, tee shirt, and whistle. He or she should be neat and clean; long hair should be tied back and kept out of the eyes. A whistle is an effective tool in conducting workouts, in starting heats of swimmers, and also signals an emergency.

A good coach lives a healthy lifestyle— gets plenty of fresh air, exercise, relaxation time and sleep, and nutritious food. I once worked with an assistant coach who smoked. He disappeared at crucial times and then returned smelling like tobacco. The children received a mixed message, as swimming and smoking contradict one another. The solution: Insist that he not smoke during practice or a meet or within range of the pool, where swimmers may see him. What he does on his own time away from the pool and the swimmers is his own business. But you have to question how good a coach can be if he smokes.

In order to be an effective coach, you need your swimmers' respect and admiration. You build trust with sincere effort and by considering your students' needs. To win their admiration, you have to be a proper role model. To have outstanding swimming ability, to have in-depth knowledge, and to be ethical and professional is admirable. The more swimmers respect and admire you, the more cooperative they will be.

Being a leader

Someone has to lead any type of organized activity. If you let the parents lead, which does happen, then the coach becomes their pawn. Parents aren't experts in swimming, don't have the credentials, experience, and knowledge that the coach has. Often a parent looks out for the interests of his or her own child rather than considering team interests. Swimming becomes political, which can dampen spirits.

If you let the swimmers lead—and there are teams where the swimmers make crucial decisions—the coach loses control. Children need mature adults to lead them. Like parents, they may consider their own interests before the groups', while a coach can and should be objective and think about what is best for everyone. Do not forget that no matter how much you have taught your swimmers about swimming and no matter how knowledgeable, experienced, and competent they become, you are still the expert and the boss. The coach is the central figure, the ultimate teacher, teaching parents, assistants, and children.

Being in control (case study #1)

I worked with an assistant coach who was a AAA age group swimmer in his youth; thus, he had knowledge and experience. But he began the season being too nice to the children, and they soon walked all over him. Once he lost control, he could never regain it. Eventually he started losing his temper and spent entire practices yelling; and the more he yelled, the worse the swimmers behaved.

He wrote a workout on the board and instead of saying, "This is it," he changed it at every child's complaint and whim.

"Oh, do we have to do four 100s?" they asked.

He erased the board and said, "Okay. Do two 100s."

Changing the workout confuses the majority of the children.

The solution: Children can be demanding. Some will try to manipulate you. You have to keep your cool and not let them get the best of you. Do not let the swimmers tell you which lane they want to swim in, who they want in their lane, and what they want their workout to be. Separate friends during workouts, especially if they focus on socializing rather than swimming.

Having confidence

If you don't have confidence in your coaching skills, then you need to develop them before becoming the head coach of a swim team. If you lack confidence due to a lack of knowledge, read books and magazines, attend clinics, attend another team's practices and observe, and then talk to other coaches. If you lack confidence due to a lack of experience, assist another coach prior to taking the lead. The best scenario is to start as a competitive swimmer and by the time you are seventeen, become a WSI. Begin teaching swimming, and after a couple of years, find work as an assistant coach, training under someone more experienced and knowledgeable and work up from there.

Case study #2

Greg, a man in his late twenties, started a swim team in a small town and then over several years built the group up to thirty interested and competent children. He had been a competitive swimmer in his youth, had been a water safety instructor for many years, became an American Red Cross instructor trainer, and also was the pool manager. Eventually, though, he left this town for a better job offer—coaching at a college. When this team was left without a coach, a parent stepped forward and said, "I will do this."

The parent became certified in CPR, First Aid, and WSI. She related to the children well and had good class management skills. Many people felt it was worth having the team with the inexperienced parent taking the lead and maybe she could evolve into a good coach. She believed that she could do this and then did the best job possible. While she did not win the top-coach-of-the-year award, with the support of those around her, she adequately led the team to their seasonal goals.

Having a positive attitude

Anyone who is leading any type of activity should be positive, especially when children are involved. Children are impressionable, and your attitude may affect the way they feel about swimming for the rest of their lives. A good coach wants to coach. You have to want to do whatever you are doing to create a positive experience. Life is full of endless possibilities for the swimmers and for you. In making choices, pick what makes you happy, not only for your own physical, mental, and emotional well-being, but also for the well-being of those around you. How can a coach be an inspiration to others if he or she is not inspired? Some people enjoy working and choose an occupation that is meaningful; others feel that no job is a good job, and they work only because they have to pay the bills. Working at a swimming pool, being a swimming coach is usually not a high-paying job. Being a coach is usually a choice, not a must.

If there is someone coaching who doesn't want to be coaching, this is an administrative problem. A possible scenario of a coach coaching and not wanting to: Your boss says, "We need a coach, and I want you to do it." You would rather perform other tasks around the pool, but if you say no, you may lose your job. First of all, feel flattered. The boss picked you out of the other workers. Then, make the best of what you are doing.

Another scenario: You enjoy the first few months of coaching, but numerous problems cause you to develop a negative attitude mid-season. Things get so difficult that you want to give your two-week notice, but no one else is available to coach. The swimmers and parents have invested in the program for the season—have paid their USA Swimming dues and bought team suits. The best choice is to finish the season, despite the problems. If you quit, you send a mixed message to the children. You want to teach them to commit to something for the season, to follow through. Another solution: Figure out what is making the job unpleasant and communicate this to a parent-support group or a boss. While the children should not be made aware of the problem, other adults may be able to help. With the help and support of others, problems can be resolved. A coach does not have to bear the burdens alone; that is why a team is a team.

A final possibility: You've been working at this same job for many years and are sick of it. But at forty years of age, you don't know what else you can do. By now you have put in your time, had your raises. Dropping this occupation and finding a new one may mean starting at the bottom of something and working your way up all over again. Instead of doing this, you opt to stay where you are, with what you know. Thus, while you have the knowledge and the experience, you lack the enthusiasm. A solution for this coach is to stay, but vary his or her methods to the point where excitement stirs within again. A coach needs to feel stimulated, because he or she is in the key position of motivating others.

To hold your swimmers' attention, you have to care about them and their learning process. Children will want to be at the pool and will be willing to listen to a coach who genuinely cares. A negative learning experience is disillusioning. While hard knocks may build character, the swimming pool should be a fun place. And also children should have a positive place where they can go, to enjoy themselves and to escape from the pressures of the world. One thing some coaches fail to realize is that swimming is not the only activity a child can do. Children choose to attend a swimming pool, and you will lose swimmers and have no team at all if you make those around you have a bad time; the child chooses the sport, but can also choose to leave it. The coach must make the experience worth staying for. If a coach feels negative about his or her job—and it may have started out positive, but turned negative because of some condition like no raise, lack of administration support, overbearing parents—she or he shouldn't be coaching, shouldn't be subjecting children who are there to learn and enjoy the learning to a bad attitude. In a situation like that, no one can succeed—or the negativity blocks the chances of success.

Wanting to be successful

This is the difference between a coach who punches a time clock and one who enjoys the job and wants to perform well. A good coach is competitive and wants to have a successful team. You have trained swimmers so they are ready for the first meet of the season. As the season progresses, you want the quality of the swim, as well as the times, to improve. If every swimmer on your team is improving, you should feel successful, whether the team or the individual wins or loses. You may be in a league where there are twelve teams and the first year you join you place twelfth. The next year you place eleventh, and the next year tenth, and so on. If individual times and team rank are continually improving, if the numbers of swimmers and interest in the sport is growing, if parental and community support is growing, you should feel successful.

Success doesn't mean winning or losing. Some people will try to make you feel as though you are not successful if you don't win. Often they are parents who must see their child winning in order to relate to the improvement as success. Each swimmer has to develop within his or her own time sequence. It's good to push a child hard, to have high expectations and standards, but you don't want to pressure him or her to the point where you create burnout. Stress is counter-productive, and the coach has to help the parents who pressure their children to see that.

Pressure can also be self-inflicted; a swimmer can be disappointed with anything he or she deems as a failure, which can be something as simple as losing a race. Teach this swimmer to swim against the clock, not others. Comparing oneself to another wastes energy and can be discouraging. Improve yourself; cut times until you reach your goal. Then set a new goal. If one swimmer focuses on another's excellence, say to him or her, "Oh, that's where you want to be? Well, *this* is where you are, and *this* is what you need to do to get *there*."

This is a valuable lesson—great things do not come easily. With natural talent, desire, and hard work, you can be as good as any hero you may have. Your hero did not attain success by sheer natural talent alone.

Committing to excellence

A good or great coach must commit to excellence, giving the job full effort. People cannot or should not expect more of you than your best. If you are knowledgeable and well-qualified, then you have the foundation needed to do the job. If the job is important to you, chances are your mind is constantly working on ways to make the team even better. Chances are, you have so many ideas that you can't wait to return to the pool to try them out. Once on the deck, you sense an urgency— with much to teach and little time—and a coach who feels differently is not doing his or her job appropriately. Time is limited when readying a team for competition.

Giving your best to each swimmer may require putting in time you don't get paid for, but you must decide whether you are going to coach the season to your fullest potential or go halfway. Perhaps you have good reason to go halfway—low pay, no administration or parent support, or uncommitted swimmers. But it's best to do the job right or not at all. If you don't give one hundred percent, how can you expect your swimmers to? If you do something halfheartedly, you limit yourself.

Building confidence in your students

A coach needs to recognize a swimmer's achievements and congratulate him or her on successes. Encouragement needs to come from someone, and when it comes from a coach it is especially motivating. The younger the swimmer the more encouragement is needed. Achievements are common at the pool; whether the steps are small or big, there is generally a movement forward.

While it is nice to get recognition, a coach cannot be expected to single someone out of a group of fifty and say, "Oh, that's the swimmer I am going to develop."

There has to be something—a desire to improve—coming from the athlete. The more a person applies himself to a task, the more others will notice. Thus, a swimmer has to win the recognition of a coach by working hard. Generally, the time and attention a coach gives to each individual swimmer should be equal in relation to the time the swimmer spends at the pool. Some swimmers work harder and longer than other swimmers and will fairly receive more time and attention.

Yet, a coach who only cares about the best swimmers on the team is not a good coach. You are going to have swimmers who range from weak to strong, but that doesn't mean your weaker swimmers won't be your strongest someday. The weak swimmers need more coaching, not to be ignored. You build a strong team by allowing for the growth of all individuals. Thus, develop each swimmer, not just those who show the most promise at the time, for all children have potential and given encouragement may surprise you.

The coach who makes each swimmer feel special is special. You can make swimmers feel good about themselves by first thinking well of them. Body language—facial expressions, hand motions—can show something you aren't saying. You have to be sincere with swimmers and sincere with yourself; you have to honestly be interested in and care about each student. Award successes, however small, and encourage your athletes to take the next step. They all have potential—a mediocre swimmer can become a good swimmer and a good swimmer can become a great swimmer.

Being fair

A coach has to divide his time evenly between swimmers and not favor one over another. You have X number of swimmers per X number of coaches and X amount of time to accomplish certain goals within a season. A coach cannot be in two places at once, to encourage or congratulate two swimmers in need, so he or she chooses one swimmer this time and the other swimmer the next.

The coach must also stay elevated in the role of the adult and not step down to become child and friend. Some children will want to be buddy-buddy with you on your free time. You can be kind to these children, but do not continually give them extra time in the pool with you alone; do not give them rides home; do not allow them to call you at home for something unimportant. The roles break down, and others on the team find this unfair. Also, you may even be interfering with the parent's relationship with the child.

If a parent is absent, and the child is reaching out for extra attention, find parents on the team to take this child under their wing, perhaps just by helping him or her get to and from practices and meets. The coach needs to focus on each individual, but not at the expense of others on the team, not by giving special attention or doing special favors, and not by getting too close. You may think you are being kind, and a supportive friend, but you need to be all those things in a professional manner and not let one child over others enter your private life, especially without placing their parents there, too.

Having good communication skills

When speaking to a group, smile and be pleasant. Use words with positive connotations, like "walk" rather than "don't run." Speak *to*, not *at* your students. Be brief and to the point. The children are there to swim, so don't make them wait through lengthy explanations. While explanation is a necessary part of teaching swimming, your students will only retain a portion of what you say. Lectures should include key words and phrases to help them focus on a particular task. Be as specific as possible, for anything that can be misinterpreted will be. Communication breaks down, because words can mean different things to different people. Choose words appropriate to the age group you are teaching; stories, examples, and figurative language will add interest. For example, the American Red Cross suggests using similes: "Kick like a dolphin."

A coach should be sensitive to each individual on the team. You should know each swimmer by name. Encourage swimmers to communicate openly with you, to share problems rather than hide them. You aren't a mind reader and cannot be expected to sense feelings that aren't expressed. But you can encourage students to feel comfortable about confiding in and putting their trust in you by reacting appropriately and in a caring way. Let them know that you are there for them, that they are what really matters. Your goal is to teach, and you should be committed to that goal. How they learn, and if they do, should be important to you. You cannot effectively teach students if you don't know what they are thinking.

The Coaching Team

The head coach

A head swimming coach coordinates the program, but may designate certain aspects of it to others—assistants, parents, or older (mature and qualified) swimmers—whom he or she must then manage. The head coach designs a block plan for the season, as well as detailed weekly and daily workout plans, and then runs practices, assigning duties to the assistant. While the best coach is on deck, actively involved and interacting with the swimmers, occasionally he or she will have an important appointment and will leave the team in the hands of a qualified assistant. By qualified I mean that the assistant has all the required certifications and is a USA Swimming coach. Whether the practices are run by the head coach or an assistant, the head coach claims responsibility for whatever happens.

The assistant coach

If you have high expectations of the way things need to be done, develop what you need and want in others rather than trying to do everything yourself. Maybe temporarily you are saving time by not training an assistant, but in the long run you are not. An assistant coach should have a competitive swimming background; should be certified in Lifeguard Training, Water Safety Instructor, CPR, and First Aid; should have teaching swimming experience; should be oriented prior to taking position on deck. It is the responsibility of the head coach to make sure assistant coaches have opportunities to learn as much as they can about technique and training. As head coach, you not only teach swimmers, but you also teach assistant coaches.

A head coach should be able to choose an assistant, someone he or she can work with. The best assistant coach you can have is one who works with you. A younger, less experienced assistant coach should not challenge a head coach. This will create conflict, which will be bad for team morale. Tell an assistant (in private) if and when he or she is out of line—for the good of the team. If the power struggle continues, this person is not right for the job and you need to find someone else.

When delegating duties to assistant coaches, allow for trial and error. Evaluate their performance in a constructive way. As they become more competent, give them more to do. We want assistant coaches to grow, to be able to handle greater responsibilities, to someday become excellent head coaches. You have to give your assistants the knowledge they need to function. When you see good results, you will know you have succeeded.

Meet with assistant coaches before or after practice to communicate seasonal, weekly, and daily plans and goals; to share the case studies of individual swimmers; and to allow them to contribute their ideas. Even though a head coach may have more knowledge and experience, recognize that each assistant brings something new to you, just as each student does, and that from each person you meet and each experience you share, you learn.

Two coaches on deck should not discuss much with each other while swimmers are in the water. Talk before or after practice, not while guarding and coaching. This is a safety issue, and also swimmers need a coach's full attention in order to get appropriate instruction. If another coach needs to talk to you while on deck, words should be brief and eyes should remain on the pool. This rule should be set down prior to the first practice and any coach who breaks it should be reminded.

Case study #3

Judy has just accepted her first job as an assistant swim coach. While she has been an American Red Cross Water Safety Instructor for one year, she is not a strong swimmer and has never been on a swim team. She is a runner and works as a grade school physical education teacher. She understands the concepts of training and competition and communicates well with the students; they like her and listen to her when she talks.

Judy calls a group of eight-and-unders to the wall, and once they line up, she tells them that it is time to do the backstroke. She then gives an incorrect explanation and demonstration of the arm stroke—something different than what she learned in her WSI course. Even though she captures her students' attention, those learning from her will not be able to intellectualize the stroke, for she hasn't intellectualized it herself.

An assistant coach should have competitive swimming experience or the head coach should train the helper appropriately, assigning tasks he or she can accomplish successfully. Present the assistant with a challenge, but supervise the activity. A proper demonstration is vital to teaching swimming. Students will model your movements. You need to move every detail of your body on deck as you want them to in the water. It is better to have a larger swimmer-to-coach ratio (no assistant) than to have an assistant who teaches incorrectly.

Co-coaching

I have worked in both head coach-assistant coach situations and in co-coaching situations and have found that establishing a clear chain of command with only one boss is preferable. Choose the most qualified coach and put him or her in charge. In a co-coaching situation, there is more potential for disharmony, which will affect team morale.

Communication becomes vital when working with someone fifty-fifty. A lot of time is spent negotiating. Both coaches must compromise equally. You may have to give up something you feel strongly about just because it is your turn to lose. Two people will normally have different ideas and coaching styles. These differences can be an asset in providing a broader view of the task at hand. But if one person gets his or her way more than the other, hard feelings can result.

The division of labor must also be fifty-fifty, or one coach will resent the other. The certification and experience level of each coach must be close to equal. A more qualified coach who has to operate on the same level as a less qualified coach can become frustrated. If either coach takes on a position of superiority, the co-coaching situation, despite who is more or less qualified, will be ruined.

Co-coaching works best if you know the person you are working with, have worked with him or her before, and know you work well together. Sometimes not even the best of friends can work together, but a valued friendship is a necessary ingredient in a successful co-coaching relationship. Two coaches must have compatible personalities and respect for one another. The friendship has to take precedence over whatever happens on the job. In the most successful co-coaching situations, I have noticed a dynamic aspect to the friendship that makes the coaches better together than alone. When the dynamics between the two coaches is right, the job is done faster and more efficiently. The energy level is usually high, as the two coaches bounce back and forth off of each other in a positive way. This is a plus for everyone on the team.

Two coaches sharing a position must be able to grow together. They must acknowledge one another's strengths and compensate for one another's weaknesses. They do not put each other down; rather, they support one another. They are not in competition; they unite and, in doing so, provide a stronger coaching front better able to do the job.

What the other coach said

Children can manipulate a situation by telling one coach that the other coach said they could do something, but the other coach is not there that day to ask. Go with your common sense. What would the other coach realistically say and do? You should know how the other coach stands on issues. Remember, the other coach is an adult and these are children who want to do what they want to do and may say anything to achieve their purpose. They may drop the name of a coach not present and say, "But Brenda said I can do this," not knowing or possibly caring if they get Brenda in trouble for saying something she didn't say. Some children (and adults) do not care whom they hurt as long as they get their way. Coaches need to stick together on the rules and negotiate philosophies, need to believe in and give each other the benefit of the doubt.

Types of coaches

An authoritarian coach has a well-behaved team. Practices run smoothly, without question or argument, so the focus can be on swimming. But this kind of coach may be disliked and may turn swimmers away from the sport. Meanwhile, the nice coach may be liked, but will be taken advantage of. A business-like coach may be too objective to connect with the individual. The team will be well-organized and updated on technique and training methods, but the individual swimmer may not feel important. The sensitive coach, on the other hand, gets too involved with the swimmers and will be hurt by someone someday. And the right-brained coach will hold creative and interesting practices, will often have a new and exciting idea to try, but teaching sessions may also be scattered and disorganized.

Chances are, you are not one type of coach, but many. You can call the different coaches within you to action in response to an occasion. For example, an intense coach may push swimmers too hard, and swimmers may burn out. An easygoing coach may not push swimmers enough, and swimmers may not reach their potential. Thus, you want to fall in-between the two extremes or be both at different times. Both can be effective in dealing with certain situations and certain individuals.

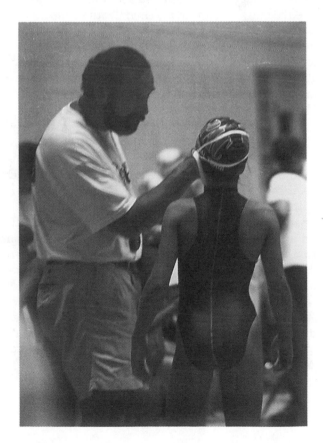

Coaching Responsibilities

Marketing your program

Recruiting is vital to the success of a swimming program. Recruiting takes time and energy and may be something a coach does not get paid for. If a coach has a parent-support group, they can participate.

Advertise the beginning of swim-team season (usually September) in the local newspaper. Hang posters around town and in the schools. Place a picture of a swimmer on the posters so those passing by who are interested in swimming will more likely notice and stop. In the article and on the posters, include practice dates, times, age and skill requirements, cost, and a phone number to call for information. Target school bulletins. If possible, give swim-team pitches to classrooms full of students, with time for questions and answers, or set up a booth in the hallway after school where students can stop for information.

At the start of the season, talk to your team and ask them to invite their friends to a practice. Let newcomers have one free day to try it out. When people call the pool, talk up the program. Have a team handbook available to give to those who drop by the pool and express an interest or know someone who might be interested. In a learn-to-swim program, you find young swimmers who come to the pool regularly for lessons and enjoy their time in the water learning. Encourage children in advanced swimming lessons to continue swimming by joining the team. Often, parents will come to you with questions, such as, "When should *Johnny* join swim team?" Or "Is *Johnny* ready?" If they don't approach you, and you see a child with potential, go to them. Encouragement from the coach and a personal invitation can instill the confidence a young swimmer may need to take the step and join.

Anytime you hold a team event, whether it be a meet, swim-a-thon, or awards' banquet, advertise in the local paper in advance and then print the results. Exposure is everything. Publicize every possible thing the team has done and is about to do. A team full of activity will appeal to many people.

Establish a relationship with your sports editor. Give him or her the meet schedule at the beginning of the season and then communicate regularly. Prior to an important event, call to remind him or her and also to extend a personal invitation. Ask for pictures to be printed as often as possible, whether the editor takes them or someone in your club does.

You may have a hard time drawing a reporter to an out-of-town meet; thus, assign a willing parent with a camera and writing skills to do the job. A team can write its own press releases, which will make the publication of team events easier; the news will more likely be printed in the time and in the way you want it to be. If a swim team wants media exposure, which means community exposure, parents need to help. Media exposure is also a good way to make those on the team feel a sense of reward for their hard work.

Publicize participation in county fairs, town parades, car washes, or bake sales. Swim team members doing fun things together will draw other children to the sport. Suits, caps, tee shirts, and jackets with the team name and logo help to spread the word that a swim team exists. If you have a local television station, air the meet. Make video tapes of the meet available to swimmers and their parents. Children who do not regularly attend the pool may view these videos and become interested in joining.

Planning the season

Plan the season far ahead of the first workout. I plan for September in May, right after the short-course season is over, while the school year is fresh in my mind and I can analyze what went well and what could have gone better. It helps to map the season out on a blank calendar.

A block plan is an overview—either of a particular season (short or long course) or a whole year. Then you divide this overview into smaller parts and are still operating within a block plan (a block of time). For example, you can divide a year into 1) pre-season; 2) pre-competitive season; 3) competitive season; 4) post-competitive season; 5) off-season. You can further divide these five seasons into weeks and each week into days. Then write a general lesson plan for each day.

Flexibility is a desirable ingredient, especially when you may not know the particular group of swimmers you will be working with until the season begins. It is like having an atlas when beginning a trip across country. You have a destination and a route, but are open to small side-trips and cannot control things like a car breaking down. Thus, while magnifying the focus, you don't completely step off the track. Once into the season, you can review the daily lesson plans at the beginning of each week and add detail. Looking ahead at a whole week you can have a pretty good feeling about the kinds of details you need to focus on, and as little things come up you can make small changes.

When planning

Determine the number of swimmers. With a large team, everyone can practice, but will have to be divided into groups defined by age and ability, depending on pool space and time and the number of qualified coaches available or affordable. You can split your team into groups of two, three, or even four. You may have only one coach, so you split your team of fifty swimmers into three groups, each group practicing at different times. This allows for more pool space, more individual attention, and a reasonable swimmer-to-coach ratio. Or you may have two groups, with twenty swimmers in each group, practicing at the same time with two coaches. You can also split these forty swimmers into three groups with three separate practice times that overlap.

When dividing your team into groups, consider the individuals involved. Consider their age: do you have mainly younger swimmers, older swimmers, or a range of ages? Consider their skill: do you have a lot of beginners or are there a lot of swimmers returning from one season to the next? There should be entry-level skill requirements to join a swim team. From that point on, you build skills. In the American Red Cross learn-to-swim program, children learn by progression. You can continue that idea in swim team by guiding swimmers step by step forward. Also consider fitness level, maturity, experience, and body size. Group those with similar abilities and of like ages together. No two athletes are physically or mentally the same. Assess the individual swimmer in the beginning of the season, during, and after; groups may need to shifted mid-season.

Determine the desired swimmer-to-coach ratio, the availability of certified, qualified coaches, and whether there's money to pay additional coaches. I suggest one coach to twenty swimmers, unless you can stagger practice time, so that you have different ages and levels coming into the pool at different times.

Consider the location. You need a pool with adequate lighting, proper ventilation, balanced chemicals, comfortable temperature, and with safety equipment easily accesible. The facility should be clean and orderly, and cleaning supplies should be present; the pool should be maintained daily. A dry, quiet office area should include a first-aid kit, a phone with emergency numbers posted, and the necessary supplies needed to conduct business.

Determine the pool size, and the space (the number of lanes) available for practices. Determine available practice times. Of the times available, which are best for the swimmers and for the coach? You have to work around school and family life. Holding practice after school, from 3-5:00 p.m. may work for children and parents, but may limit the choice of coaches. Practicing from 5-6:30 p.m. opens options, for a person can work a full-time job and coach after work. A coaching job is usually not full-time, but can work well with a pool manager, swim instructor, or lifeguarding position.

Determine administrative support. Does the pool cater to everyone, or to a particular group, such as adults or children; lap or recreation swimmers; those in lessons or those on a team? For example, a pool in a retirement community generally caters to the senior population, not a youth swim team. If all groups are included, are the time slots available for usage balanced? How rigid or flexible is the system? Often, people get into a routine; sometimes changing the pool schedule is the appropriate answer, but it is disruptive to those employers, employees, and patrons set in their ways. The schedule should be experimented with to accommodate the largest number of people. If someone complains, evaluate the numbers who are satisfied, the numbers dissatisfied, and gear your schedule to demand. All systems need to analyze success and failure and re-adapt the schedule accordingly. What works should be continued, despite the political interests of a particular group.

Determine the number of sessions (daily and weekly) and the duration of each practice. Three times per week is the minimum you want your team to practice. Five days a week is preferable for swimmers over ten years of age, if they want to have a chance in competition. A swimmer should take off at least one day a week, so his or her body can rest and recover. Should the team practice over vacation? This depends on the team and its goals and the meet dates. All swimmers benefit from rest and time off. Swimmers can practice individually over a vacation, and having the motivation to do this builds self-confidence.

Determine participant fees for a season. Assess the costs to run the program and then set a realistic and affordable price. Besides coaching and possibly pool-rental fees, there are club, coach, and swimmer fees to join USA Swimming. If you do not have a parent-support group, who will pay the club fee for your team to join USA Swimming? Other fees (usually paid by the individual, not the club) include meet, travel, and personal equipment fees.

The competitive swim program will never be simple, but you can strive to keep it as simple as possible. This is not always easy when you are dealing with many different ages and levels of swimmers and a variety of personalities.

Setting policy

Your team can go by a strict, flexible, or middle-of-the-road policy. The approach you take will depend on the age, skill, maturity level of the group. A mature, motivated group may handle flexibility well while a group of young, wild children will need structure in order to stay on track.

Policy will also depend on who is in charge—the parents, pool administrator, or you. If you are in charge, you can set some standards that go along with your philosophies. If the parents are in charge, you have to work with them, but because you are the head coach, your opinion does carry weight. The coach needs to believe in what he or she is enforcing.

Policies need to be set anticipating particular problems, such as what to do when children arrive late or leave early. Maybe you want to be flexible, maybe not, but you need to tell the team ahead of time what the consequences will be, so that they know what to expect and what to do should they find themselves in that situation. I recommend that they not be allowed to interrupt the practice with questions about what they have missed. They also need to warm up before joining the workout.

If a swimmer is consistently late, pull him or her aside and ask why. Can anything be done to correct this? Stress the importance of being on time. Each practice is crammed with necessary activity and learning. It is counterproductive for a coach to be staying after practice all the time to make up what others have missed. Once in awhile is okay, but this can get out of hand. You also need to communicate with the parents—for what if the parents think the child is in practice and on time and he or she is not? You need to know that the parents know what is going on. If a parent talks to you about a dentist appointment that will interfere with a child's punctuality, that's understood and the exception is made.

If you feel strongly about certain policies in terms of lateness, leaving early, and missing practice, you need to put them in writing in a team handbook. Half the time the parents don't even read the handbook, but if there is a problem or discrepancy regarding what you said or didn't say, you can pull out the book and then stand by it. Whatever you say can and often will be misinterpreted--or changed if it doesn't fit someone's program. Thus, communicate clearly both verbally and in writing, and be prepared for people to challenge what you have to say. Nonetheless, in order to have an organized swim team, and to organize a group of children, you have to have rules to keep things consistent and non-chaotic.

Swim or don't come (case study #4)

Joe arrives at the pool, but has excuses as to why he cannot work out that day. You ask him to call his parents for a ride home, and he tells you they aren't home. You are the only coach on deck with twenty-five swimmers in the water and do not have time to call the parents yourself. You ask him to sit on the bleachers, which he does. But then when your back is turned, he walks across the deck. You end up spending more time with this swimmer who is not swimming than with those in the water.

Distracting a coach takes time away from those who are participating and becomes a safety issue as well; thus, set a policy that addresses this possible problem.

Paying dues (case study #5)

Parents not paying their monthly dues on time, or at all, was a continual problem while Amber was coaching. The season began in September, and all parents paid the first month, since they had to sign up their child. During sign-up and through monthly newsletters, parents were informed of payment amounts and dates. In October, some people didn't pay and were billed. By November and December, over half the team didn't pay and were billed. By Christmas break, negligent parents owed the pool two hundred dollars in back dues. Amber complained to her boss repeatedly about people not paying dues. He told her that she was doing a great job and to continue to do the best that she could. Thus, Amber was in a situation that was causing her stress, and her boss helped her to deal with the stress by being supportive of her.

The solution: those who pay swim. Swimmers who attend without paying require attention that should be given to those who pay. Also, by setting standards of payment and practice, you establish the groundwork for a bigger team going in the right direction someday. To be answered by each club: How long should unpaid dues be allowed? Should there be a family rate for families with more than one child?

Meet deadlines (case study #6)

You've sent a newsletter to all parents, and then verbally told both swimmers and parents that meet fees are due by a certain date. You also gave them this information on registration day when you handed them the team booklet with meet dates and fee deadlines. What if fees are not paid by the deadline? You have to sign up your team, mail the host club a list of swimmers and a check, by a certain date.

You have several options: 1) Call the parents and get a verbal commitment. Ask for the money by the following practice. But keep in mind that you may not collect one-hundred percent of the money promised. 2) Establish a policy: Those who sign up by the deadline go to the meet; those who miss the deadline miss the meet and will try harder next time. Allowing parents to pay late, or you paying for your swimmers to participate with a verbal commitment that their parents will pay you back, only allows people to get away with what they can--a pattern that can easily continue. If you don't allow the pattern to develop in the first place, a swimmer may miss a meet or two, but will eventually get on track, and you will have a team that follows deadlines rather than a team that doesn't take you seriously. This will save you time in the long run. Do you really want to be calling parents every time there's a meet, or billing those who don't pay? As the cliché goes, they snooze, they lose. 3) Each swimmer pays for all the meets that season when they register. For example, if eight meets are scheduled from September-January and meet fees average between eight to twelve dollars per swimmer, depending on the number of events they swim, find a reasonable average—say, ten dollars per meet. Charge each swimmer eighty dollars in September to cover meet costs for the season. This will encourage swimmers to attend all meets—which is what you want anyway—for they have paid in advance.

Orientation day

It is a good idea to have an orientation or registration day. Invite all of the swimmers, not just those who are new, and extend the invitation to parents, too. This is a way for everyone to get to know you and each other better. Introduce all of the coaches and relate their swimming experience and credentials. Discuss team policies and procedures, the season schedule, how practices will be structured, and the division of swimmers into ages and levels. Distribute a handbook, where you have put all of this into writing. Stress the importance of swimmers committing for the season; explain that a swimmer cannot understand his or her potential unless at least one season of work is given.

Ask the swimmers to sign their name, address, phone number, and birth date on a list or index card that you may later type into a computer. You need their address to mail newsletters, team information, or bills; their phone number to call their parents if there is a problem, or to call them if a meet or practice is cancelled; and their birth date, so you will be sure to swim them in the right age group at all times.

Should you have tryouts? This depends on your community size and how many children will be interested and turn out for the team. It depends on how much pool time and space you have, how much money can be spent on coaches, and how many coaches are available. If time, space, coaches, and money are limited, you will have to set a maximum number of swimmers to take. Gauge whether you should have tryouts by what has happened in the past. Tryouts are often based on having a minimum skill level, and this is important. And if you need to divide your swimmers into two or three groups based on ability, you need to see the children swim.

Analyzing the swimmer

At the beginning of the swim season, analyze the strengths and weaknesses of each swimmer on the team. If it helps, write a case history of each athlete and add to it as the season progresses, constantly re-evaluating technique, training, and performance. Where is this individual in his or her development? What does he or she need to work on most? What can you immediately do to motivate this swimmer? Take into consideration each child's age and personality, not just his or her level of swimming.

When assessing the potential of an individual, you must look at where he or she is developmentally and determine a realistic goal for the season. Age and skill play a part, as well as the time you have to work with this swimmer. It is best to focus primarily on seasonal goals. There can be smaller or larger goals, but one season, that one block, is something both coach and swimmer should be able commit to and set out to accomplish.

If you look at accomplishment as a straight line, compare the point where the swimmer is to the point where the swimmer wants to go. If this goal is not realistic, the coach needs to lower the swimmer's expectations; and if the vision seems too low, both coach and swimmer need to shoot higher. Each day that an individual goes to the pool he or she has a current position on that line, which should at some rate be moving forward. Within that point, though, there is a high and low range. When the athlete participates in a meet, the goal is for him or her to perform at the high end of this range.

Teaching the swimmer

A coach is responsible for the education of the student and must do everything possible to ensure that the environment is conducive to learning. This means minimizing distractions in and around the pool. A child may be distracted, for example, if the air or water temperature is too hot or too cold, if there are other noisy activities nearby making it difficult to hear the coach, or if non-participating patrons, including parents, are allowed on deck and can speak to or holler at *Johnny* any time.

The coach is responsible for the mental, physical, and emotional development of the swimmer. A coach's ultimate goal should be that the swimmer learn and improve. He or she must teach the proper mechanics and make sure that the information, besides being correct, is also current. Coaches need to train swimmers according to age, ability, the time of season, and also consider their goals and needs. A coach must also ready athletes, both mentally and physically, for competition by teaching the strategies of the sport.

Maintaining records

Maintaining records, while often a lot of work, provides the coach with information that may be vital to his analysis of the swimmers and their progress. The head coach is ultimately responsible for every job that needs to be done. Even if you have a strong parent support group, you never know when some complication will occur; you need to know what jobs are getting done when and by who, so that you can step in when necessary.

Health and Safety Record: You need to know if one of your athletes has a medical condition that will either affect his or her performance or that you need to consider when training. An athlete with a medical problem may reach the same end as any other athlete, but may need different considerations or practice strategies in the process. You also need an emergency information card, so that you know who to contact in case of an injury or sudden illness. Even though you are protected under the Good Samaritan Law when you follow the Emergency Action Plan (check, call, care) and provide care in accordance with your level of training, as required by your job, it is important to have parents complete a form in the beginning of the season, giving their consent for you to give first aid, if needed, to their child.

Accident report forms should be available at the pool in case of an accident and then filled out promptly. When an accident occurs, employees on the scene who aided in the rescue, patrons who witnessed the event, and even the victim can provide details about what happened. If this information is ever needed, it is easier and more accurate to obtain immediately after the accident occurs; later, witnesses may be gone. Record the date and time of the accident; the names, addresses, and phone numbers of all those interviewed; and record fact, not opinion.

Attendance Record: Attendance is important; how can a student improve at a sufficient pace if he or she does not participate on a regular basis? While you may be able to keep a child's attendance in your head in a general sense, you cannot be exact in terms of counting practices attended and missed, and you may need that specific information, especially when analyzing a student's progress. A parent may want to know why their child isn't progressing as much as the other children, and it may be due to attendance. Also, a parent may need to know if a child attended on a particular day. If a parent asks you on a Friday what happened on a Monday or Tuesday, and you have fifty swimmers on your team, you may be thankful for that attendance book.

Practice Record: You can look back on what swimmers did in a workout a month ago or a year ago to determine if you are currently gauging yardage and focus appropriately.

Progress Record: Charts showing the swimmers' progress can be motivational. Regularly time your swimmers and keep track of their progress. When a swimmer breaks a previous time and progresses one step, however small or big, praise the accomplishment and encourage him or her to move on to the next step. In a meet, both the coach and swimmer should know the personal best the swimmer is trying to break. Record progress in a notebook—weekly, monthly, and seasonally. Tie one season to the next. Look at a swimmer's progress over the years. If one coach leaves, the records should be passed on to the next coach. Let each swimmer look at his or her times, but no one else's. Or you can hand out progress reports, listing the events and all the times set at meets that season. Age-group swimmers usually do improve, so this can be encouraging.

Young swimmers who don't have technique down will cut times in leaps as they improve strokes, starts, and turns. Once they grasp stroke technique, which is a never ending learning process, they improve with training, physical growth, and emotional maturity. Then the emphasis should be on how hard they work. How hard and long can they train and how much can they push themselves or be pushed by a coach before they burn out or resist? They have to return to their goal and give one-hundred percent if they want to reach it, and as a coach you need to be there to encourage them every step of the way.

Charting progress (case study #7)

At the end of every practice, Patrick stood in the office for an hour, answering questions from parents and swimmers, collecting money, and marking each swimmer's yardage on an American Red Cross fifty mile swim chart. Everything you do with your athletes, he had heard, you must record. So he charted not only their times, but also their attendance and their yardage per practice.

He had asked his swimmers to mark in their own miles, but they often forgot, and he wouldn't get an accurate record unless he did this for them. Clocking their yardage was helpful, but it seemed he was the only one interested in the swimmers reaching fifty miles and getting an award for this at the end of the season. One day he took the chart down, and no one noticed.

When Patrick was an age-group swimmer, the mileage chart had motivated him. Often what worked for you as an age-group swimmer may not work for those you are coaching. Yet it is always worth giving your ideas a try to find out what does and doesn't work.

Ordering equipment

A coach should order equipment such as kickboards, backstroke flags, stopwatches, but should avoid ordering personal equipment such as suits, caps, and goggles. Give this job to a parent or local sport shop.

Whether your team orders the team suit out of a catalogue or whether you go through a local sports shop is up to you. It took me a few years of coaching to figure out that I preferred the local sport shop. The parents thought we could save money by ordering through a catalogue, yet no one volunteered to help me. This required a lot of work, which wasn't part of my job description and which I did not get paid for. Suddenly I had to fit the swimmers, take orders, collect money, and then pay the invoice—and deal with any other little problems that occurred in the process, such as a suit arriving, but not fitting, and then needing to be returned and exchanged for another. I finally went to the local sport shop, and they did all of this for me. The sports shop obtained the suits wholesale and sold them to us for the retail price plus a team discount, which equaled the price we paid shopping through a catalogue.

Organizing an awards banquet (case study #8)

The 1981 minutes of a PTSC parent meeting reads, "Our season's finale turned into a disaster. I mailed announcements before leaving town, prior to the potluck, and while I was gone someone changed the date of the banquet. Half of the swimmers arrived one evening for a potluck without awards and the other half came the following night and attended a potluck banquet with awards. Since I was gone, I didn't help Laurie with the awards, and she didn't ask for money to purchase material. Her finances allowed for seven small trophies engraved with funny remarks. The whole idea for this banquet was to give a lot of funny awards to all the children."

There are several problems with this scenario: While it is nice for every child to get something at the awards ceremony, trophies should be special and limited to those who show extraordinary effort and perform especially well in a given season. Also, the parent and coach did not communicate properly. The parent in charge went away at the wrong time; she should have scheduled this event at a time when she knew she would be present. If she did have to leave, she should have made sure before she left that someone was taking over the job. The ceremony should have been laid out—what awards were to be given and to whom, who was ordering, how much money would be spent, and how the bill would get paid. Even though it is nice to have a parent-support group, the coach should oversee all activities and be willing to jump in should a parent fail to do a job properly. The coach continues to manage, while the parent helps.

Coaching Factors

Population density

Coaching in a populated area has advantages. The more swimmers a coach has to draw upon and develop, the more events can be filled at a meet. Often this means you can swim more relays, which may be your edge over another team. Getting to practice may be easier for those who live in the city or suburb; attendance may be better. Even if parents cannot transport children to and from practice, buses can get them there. Your swimmers are more likely to turn out for meets, because travel time to other pools is less.

Coaching in a rural area can be more difficult. The numbers of swimmers per age group is limited. Sometimes you do not have enough swimmers to fill the events. You can lose a lot of points in a meet just from your no-entries. There are not many older swimmers on the team; those who are fast have no competition in practice to push them harder than the clock and the coach, which is often not the same as a swimmer in the next lane. While transportation to practices may not be a problem, meets are far away, require extensive travel, and not everyone on your team will commit to that.

Affordability

The costs of being on a swim team include monthly dues, meet fees, travel and food money to meets, practice and team suits, a cap, goggles, and a towel. In an affluent area, parents pay the price in a timely fashion and that's it; no extra thought or energy is spent in that direction. In a poor area, swimmers may lack the proper equipment, such as goggles or a cap. Parents may not pay dues or meet money in a timely fashion or at all. Much effort may be spent billing and re-billing parents who don't pay on time.

Solution: You have to make payment policies and stick with them, even if you have a swimmer who has tremendous potential. You can offer scholarships to low-income families or encourage sponsors. If the parent still does not pay after many chances and offers, that is too bad for the child, but you have to stick to payment rules or you will have a larger problem with many people taking advantage. Thus, because of money, you may have to let a good swimmer go and you may have a smaller team. A swimmer or a family needs to be able to afford team dues, meet fees, and equipment costs. This may seem minor, but a family with numerous children on a fixed low income may struggle to pay what is required. Once the child excels, participating in regional, zone, or even national meets may become more difficult, because costs increase.

Community interest (case study #9)

Jeff coaches swimming at a large, new indoor recreation facility in a retirement community. The twenty-five-yard, six-lane pool ranges in depth from three feet at one end to twelve feet at the other. During swim team practice, three lanes are used while the other half of the pool is divided into two sections, one for diving (a diving board is mounted on the deck and hangs above the deep end) and one for recreation. Separate pools (one for wading and one for hot tubbing) and a sauna are heavily in use during swim team practice. The facility also offers two large weight rooms, exercise rooms and aerobic classes, and racquetball courts.

The focus of the aquatic center is on recreation, not competition. The team is never in the water by themselves. Because the aquatic center caters to a retired population, pool time for youth activities is limited to three days a week. Water exercise, laps, and therapeutic swims take precedence. Thus, the team is small, and it is hard for them to be competitive with other teams that practice five days a week. But the children on the team are learning and becoming better and stronger swimmers.

I contrast this scenario with another small town thirty miles away that consists of all ages of people, but seems to also contain a lot of young families with children. Parents often comment that this is a nice—safe and affordable— community in which to raise children. There is one pool in the town (located on school grounds), and the focus is on teaching children to swim. This begins with the American Red Cross Infant/Preschool Aquatic Program, and a child can climb the levels and move into an active youth swim team. The swim team has priority over other programs and occupies the entire pool during a prime time, from 2:30 to 5:00 p.m. five days a week. During the day the school uses the pool to teach swimming to children, and community lessons and recreation swims are held at night—except in the summertime, when the schedule completely changes. Adult lap and aqua-aerobic classes are scheduled for an hour here and there in-between the youth programs.

When these two community swim teams compete in a dual meet, it is obvious which team has the greatest chance for success. One community is focused on its youth and the other on the elderly. Each pool program addresses the needs of the community by serving a majority. Thus, you may want to assess the community that you are coaching in and tailor both your goals and expectations to fit the need.

Organization

A common problem with many working situations is that employer and employee are at odds. I have rarely worked in a situation where employees haven't complained about their boss. Employees seem to feel they deserve more than they are getting, and employers do not feel they are getting adequate productivity. Employees can afford to stand around, take long breaks, and work slowly because it's not their dollar. Meanwhile, employers are burdened by excessive taxation, making it difficult to make ends meet. Or the employee criticizes the way the employer wants the job done, even though the employer is footing the bill and has a right to have his or her way. Employees rebel because they feel trapped in this subordinate situation.

The best working relationship occurs when employers encourage employees with reasonable wages, periodic raises, pleasant working conditions, and an open line of communication— treating them like allies, or part of a team. Having a job can be a privilege, but only if the job is enjoyable, only if you are appreciated, only if you are challenged to perform well. Thus, a positive work environment rests in the hands of the employer.

What does this have to do with working at a swimming pool? We know that swimming is fun, but even at a pool, politics can keep things from running smoothly. This can infect all of the programs, even a swim team. A pool needs a chain of command. Each person in that chain has important duties to fulfill.

Destructive comments about the administration or another employee destroys organization. When a coach passes blame to a manager in front of a swim team parent, for example, the damage is done. Talking behind a boss's back is destructive; nothing can be done to resolve the conflict, and you have created more negativity. The coach should support the organization he or she works for, especially in front of patrons.

What if you confront your boss when you feel strongly about something, and he doesn't listen or does listen but does nothing? What if you know you are right about something, like no diving into the shallow end; what if he is allowing this? Put your concern in writing, not only to him, but to others involved. This will protect you should an accident occur, and it may create change.

A non-supportive administration (case study #10)

Sara is only paid for her time on deck coaching, but is expected to do the extras—order team suits, keep attendance and payment records, bill parents who don't pay on time, and more. She tries to delegate duties to parents, but because there is no parent-support group, no one steps forward. Jobs need to be done, so she does them, and the parents think she is paid for the extras, that they are part of her job. She grows bitter because the administration is unsupportive and expects her to work for free.

She has worked at the pool for five years, for six dollars an hour, without a raise, so she confronts her boss with the big question. Her boss, the recreation supervisor, tells her that basketball, baseball, and soccer coaches do not get paid, that she should feel lucky that she does. She argues that the basketball, baseball, and soccer coaches are recreation-sponsored, in-town little league teams coached by parents. The swim team is affiliated with USA Swimming and travels to other towns to compete. If he doesn't pay a swim team coach, he still has to pay a lifeguard, for swimmers can't swim without a lifeguard on duty. Sara is both a coach and lifeguard.

He then says that the focus should be on a swim *club*, not a swim *team*. Youngsters come to the pool to swim laps and improve. He does not want to pay extra for time spent going to meets and "if a swimmer wants a competitive situation, he or she can move to the city." She argues that many great swimmers come from small towns, that there is interest in competitive swimming in their community, and that many youngsters need competitive goals to make practice more meaningful.

In the end, Sara receives a twenty-five-cent raise.

Solution: Sara needs a parent-support group. This needs to be everyone's team, not just hers, and then these jobs become everyone's responsibility. An active parent-support group can fight the administration for her, can insure that she is paid for extras or can take the burden off of her by working themselves. If there is interest in competitive swimming in the community, and the man in control is blocking progress, those who are interested need to unite and step forward.

Hours and pay

What you are paid influences your attitude and can influence how much time you are willing to commit. What do your duties entail per wage? Too many volunteer expectations can lead to a bad attitude, especially if the parents think you are getting paid for a particular task and it is really an extra that either they should be doing or no one should be doing. Consider salary before accepting a coaching job. Consider the duties that the job requires per wage. If you accept the job and then later find that there are tasks that you aren't paid for that need to be done, you may find yourself in an unsatisfying situation that you are committed to for a season. In that case, you must make the best of it.

Also consider the working hours, for generally coaching jobs are part-time positions. Practices usually occur five afternoons a week, with meets on weekends. Parent groups or league meetings often take place in the evenings—and sometimes you must travel out of town, leaving as early as 5:00 a.m. and returning as late as 10:00 p.m. Perhaps you are employed at the pool full-time, performing other duties in conjunction with coaching. If not, very likely you are juggling coaching with another job. Since swim team practices are often held in the late afternoon (this works best for the swimming families), coaching does not always correlate with the typical 9-5:00 job. The team is often so demanding that you have little time for your own recreation, especially if you have a family life to juggle as well. You need to decide before you take a coaching job if you are willing to give your time this extensively and if working part-time is acceptable.

A coach's age

Coaches in their twenties are generally idealistic. They compensate for lack of experience with an abundance of energy. And children easily identify with them. Young coaches may make mistakes, but can chalk it up to learning, bounce back, and move on. They can easily motivate others, for they are motivated themselves. When a coach nears thirty, expectations increase, but so does maturity and experience. Often, these coaches already have or are starting families of their own, so they easily win the approval of parents. That the coach is also a family person provides common ground.

A forty-year-old often needs to make more money to make a job worthwhile. A coach at this age has experience that needs to be worth something. Also, while in your twenties and thirties you had time to waste, now time feels as though it's running out, and if you have dreams to accomplish, you have to focus on them; you become more serious. If coaching is the dream, you have probably already created a good team at this point or secured a job on an established team that has hired you because you are good.

While age is relative and some children may not be able to tell the difference between a coach who is twenty, thirty, or forty, patience and energy wane with age while experience and knowledge increase.

Male and female coaches

While there is an increasing number of women athletes and coaches and more opportunities than ever for women in the world today, I believe that most swimmers and parents still prefer a male head coach. Why?

Historical factors: Currently, girls and young women are being offered a wide range of sports, more than in past generations. I was an age-group swimmer in the sixties, and all of my coaches, until I reached college, were men. In college, swim team was divided into male and female; the female team practiced with a female coach, the male team with a male coach. Competitions were also segregated. This is still true of college swimming today.

Sociological factors: 1) Because of the number of divorces and the lack of a father figure for many, a male coach attracts and influences young children, especially if he is a good role model and can give children from broken families a direction; 2) Even in the nineties, men are still, deep in our psyches, considered to be superior in sports. Despite the fallacy (when considering the spectrum of sport), many people are still prejudiced. And women swimmers, while close to men, still do not stand a chance when competing with them; 3) Parents grew up with male coaches and male role models influencing sport. They, like their children, need a leader and a role model, someone to depend on, to be assured that this will be a positive experience for the entire family. While the swimmer practices with the team, the meets often become a family event as well as families meeting with other families, who become, through swimming, friends; 4) The male athlete seems to thrive with a male coach more than with a female coach; female athletes will benefit from either. I have noticed, though, that women swim instructors experience more success than men in the learn-to-swim levels, especially levels 1-3. Thus, in competitive swimming, I believe it is safe to say that many women coaches may relate best with eight-and-under and ten-and-under age groups. The best scenario is to have a coaching team that combines both sexes, so that a child can go to either for a particular problem.

Psychological factors: Coaching is an emotionally stressful job. Women are generally more emotional than men. Men are more likely to put personal feelings aside for professionalism. Men are less likely to lose sleep if someone doesn't like them or the way they do things. Women worry more, internalize the hardships, and burn out faster. A coach must be tough, not sensitive. A sensitive coach will not survive. A successful woman coach must have a dominant, forceful personality.

The 1990s

It was easier to teach swimming to children in the 1970s and 1980s than in the 1990s. While in the 1990s we have more information available to us on techniques and training that will make swimmers faster, we also have to deal with behavior problems we didn't have to deal with in the past to the extreme that we have to deal with them now.

Raising a child in the 1990s is difficult. Economic pressures often weaken the family unit. Both parents leave home to work, to afford material things for the family, yet in doing so create an absence of emotional and spiritual comfort. While both parents are working, children are placed in the hands of baby-sitters, older siblings, or day-care providers. Sending children to school relieves some of the economic pressure, in not having to pay for a baby-sitter, but this has given the schools more power and say in the raising of "society's children."

Separation and divorce are commonplace and are often a result of economics rather than incompatibility. In the absence of parents, children rely heavily on friends. Yet children need adult supervision, as well as guidance in making decisions. An academic institution lacks the compassion of a true parent and may be instrumental in creating a less emotional, even violent youth.

Penelope Leach states in her book *Children First*, "Our society has devalued parents to such an extent that individual good parenting is not only exceedingly difficult, but ultimately insufficient" (xiii). She also says, "...the less time parents and children spend together, and the fewer thoughts and activities they share, the more powerful secondary influences are likely to be" (23).

Television watching is one of those influences that seems to have an adverse effect on children. Television watching fosters passivity, inactivity, instant gratification (which hinders the development of a child's attention span), and a self-centeredness, which then causes behavior problems in children. Television shows and advertisements contribute to materialism and can seduce youngsters, making them want more. The young, growing child cannot differentiate between what is good or bad for him or her. And in the absence of parents, who can supervise healthy activities, children become exposed to the evils of society. Children are made to believe they are as smart, if not smarter than any grown-up, which creates dissension between parents and youth. The mass media seems to be intentionally dismantling the family unit by further creating mistrust in parents while parents are gone, and for the sole purpose of giving *it* (society) the ultimate control.

Bringing a child into the world is a serious responsibility and a challenge as well. The parent has to be attentive, creative, and as strong-willed as any outsider in asserting what is best for the child. The coach's role is more important than ever as young children try to make sense of a fast-paced, complicated world. Children need positive adult role models. They need to know that there is a place to go in the world where they will receive proper guidance and some stability. What healthier place than the swimming pool? What better person than the right coach, a coach who teaches commitment, discipline, and sportsmanship.

As a coach, it is hard not to be concerned about the world in which your swimmers are growing up. While the world moves more and more quickly and many material things become instantly attainable, success as a swimmer takes concentration and effort. If it is true that "Increasingly, adolescents--and many of the rest of us, as well--too often want it all, want it now, and want it without effort" (Wagner 256), then swim team is a good place for children to learn that they have to work hard for rewards and that this takes time. If children have become more passive from watching too much television, in swim team they learn that in order to win they will have to strive aggressively. And, if they come to practice angry or sad and put these emotions into the water along with their bodies, after an hour of swimming, they will feel a lot better.

Children today have many choices. It is important for them to try many things, to discover what they enjoy or are good at. And what they enjoy they usually become good at, because they tune in and give time to the task. Those who stick with swimming, even for a whole season, are the ones who enjoy it; they are there not because they have to be, but because they want to be.

Burnout (case study #11)

Summer swim team ends in July, and after coaching intensively since September without a break, Lisa is exhausted. Before she has time to take a vacation, her boss wants her to commit to the following season. Lisa questions whether she should. Once she makes the commitment, there seems to be no way out until the following July. The team is so demanding that other aspects of her life are neglected. She has no weekends and has evening meetings to attend on top of afternoon practices—all for a part-time job that doesn't pay well. She does commit and continues to commit for six years, but each year her energy wanes. She is unable to take a long enough break and never completely recovers from one season to the next. She enters each season a little less enthusiastically.

Solution #1: Find a new occupation.

Solution #2: Challenge yourself by restructuring the program. Set goals for the coming season and think of one season at a time; make each season better than the last. Also, ask for more hours and a raise.

Solution #3: Instead of deciding whether to coach for another year, why not commit to one season? A pool could have a few coaches on hand and rotate every three months. Children join in the fall, winter, spring, or summer, and each season has a different coach with fresh energy. And it is good for swimmers to be exposed to different coaches, even if they bond best with a particular one.

Factors that lead to burnout

- being idealistic
- expecting more and getting less
- having to spend too much time on discipline
- low pay
- part-time rather than full-time work
- practice times in the middle of the day
- a critical rather than supportive parent group or administration
- fellow employees, who step on toes to get ahead or pass the buck
- being over-qualified
- working too hard for too long and not taking breaks

Symptoms of burnout

- a negative attitude
- cynicism
- feeling helpless or ineffective
- emotional exhaustion
- lack of personal accomplishment
- impersonalization
- physical health deteriorates
- psychosomatic illness
- insomnia
- poor work performance
- absenteeism
- relationships deteriorate

First aid for burnout

- think positively; control negative thoughts and feelings
- analyze the *level* of stress you are experiencing
- determine the *cause* of the stress
- learn productive ways of coping with stress: massage, hot tub/sauna, meditation
- rest and relax; do what you enjoy outside of the pool (read, play tennis, go camping)
- separate professional and personal life
- find others to give you support

PART TWO

The Age-Group Swimmer

When a child first joins the team, the coach assesses his or her skill level, assigning a group and a lane. At this point, the coach only vaguely knows the child, but that will change with time. Each swimmer is an individual and differs physically, mentally, and emotionally.

Even though a swimmer practices with other swimmers, much of his or her time is spent in silent meditation. While isolated within a fluid element, body and mind work as one. Swimmers meet before and after swims, each with differing thoughts, feelings, physical abilities, life experiences, and interests. Swimming—something they all do—is the common denominator.

The dynamics of a team change seasonally, as participants come and go. The team depends on what each athlete brings to the whole—on the way individuals interact and work together. Swimmers compete in age groups—as eight-and-unders, ten-and-unders, twelve-and-unders, fourteen-and-unders, and nineteen-and-unders. Climbing up the age group ladder, they are involved in a developmental process, maturing and moving closer to full potential.

Commitment

No matter what the child's age, joining a team is an act of commitment. The longer the commitment, the more skilled the athlete becomes. Returning to an activity on a regular basis—so many times a week, year after year—requires dedication. A true swimmer wants to be at the pool and is drawn back again and again.

The individuals on your team will have different levels of commitment, ranging from swimming being one of many things in their lives to swimming being the most important thing. Some swimmers do everything possible to succeed; others just want to be part of the team and have fun. Some choose to swim; others are forced. Some give the minimum; others give the maximum. Some have natural talent; others have to work hard to succeed. But whatever pushes someone to want to be a good swimmer comes from within. A swimmer must apply full effort in order to realize his or her potential. The greatest swimmers have a desire to excel and push for excellence.

Attitude

It's important to give youngsters a positive beginning in a sport so they will want to return, for only in returning can they evolve into better athletes. A coach should encourage those he or she is coaching—regardless of their age—and give them the most positive experience possible.

Athletes with positive attitudes work better than those with negative attitudes. Once an experience turns negative, learning and productivity slow down. The athlete lacks spirit, doesn't feel motivated, and thus will not push himself, will have to be pushed. The individual is less likely to achieve his or her potential, and the team as a whole does not move forward as efficiently as

A Positive Attitude...

stems from:
• receiving encouragement from swim teachers, coaches, and parents;
• having role models, such as coaches, older athletes who are admirable and present the younger athlete with a positive image, and swimming heroes (like the Olympians);
• getting along with your peers;
• enjoying the competitive experience, no matter the outcome.

A Negative Attitude...

results from external and (or) internal pressure.

<u>External pressures</u>:
• critical or judgmental adults;
• unsupportive parents;
• conflicts with your peers;
• other people having expectations of you that you can't or don't want to meet;
• being forced to participate.

<u>Internal pressures</u>:
• setting personal goals too high, expecting too much of yourself;
• pushing too hard and burning out;
• conflicts regarding participation;
• feeling guilty over not giving one-hundred percent, comparing results to potential;
• being disappointed with your performance;
• feeling anxious about competition;
• the inability to communicate when things go wrong.

it could. An athlete with a negative attitude may experience success, but can hurt others —and the sport—in the process. Because the athlete is stressed out, he or she will not be able to enjoy the game.

In this situation, the coach and athlete need to step back and analyze what is wrong and how it can be corrected. Let the athlete know that he or she can talk to you, that you care and can help. A swimmer says, "Look at all the things I have against me" when he should be saying "look at all the things I have going for me."

Burnout

Anyone who returns to the pool day after day, week after week will experience a lull now and then. Stress can result from a poor diet, lack of sleep, tense moments (like a fight with a friend), outside pressures accumulating (being involved in too many activities), or fighting an illness. A coach needs to recognize when a swimmer is not as perky as usual and cut back on the yardage temporarily.

First-degree stress: As the swimmer progresses through the season, more yardage is added. There should always be a minimum and maximum yardage set for any particular point in the season. A stressed swimmer usually feels better, both physically and mentally, if he or she does something rather than nothing. But if he or she does not cut back on structured, mandatory activities that require concentration and effort, then second-degree stress may develop. Symptoms of first-degree stress are irritability, frustration, and repetitive worrying. But once rested, the tense or tired swimmer will bounce back.

Second-degree stress: The swimmer is exhausted, cynical, and moody. A week or a month off in the middle of the competitive season can set a swimmer back; yet if the body and the mind are signaling that something is wrong, easing back is the best answer, for once a swimmer regains energy and attitude, success is more likely.

Third-degree stress: If the swimmer continues to push or be pushed while feeling low, stress can turn into full-blown burnout, which may or may not be cured. The swimmer may drop out completely or make it to the end of the season in a depression. You may see the swimmer the following season, but the memory of the experience is there; something has been lost that will be difficult to regain. The child does not return to the sport with the same mental or physical energy. Burnout may not be an immediate, but an aftereffect, something that hits the swimmer after all the striving for some particular goal is over. Also, if the stakes are set too high—if the swimmer has worked to the point of no return and sacrificed other things in his or her life—he or she may be disappointed if the outcome of a particular competition doesn't match expectations.

Burnout is a dangerous condition that needs immediate attention for the good of the individual experiencing the symptoms and for those around him or her. It is important for both coach and swimmer to be able to recognize and treat stress before full blow burnout occurs. Symptoms include: reduced self-esteem, withdrawal from others, physical pains, and breathing difficulty. First aid for burnout: Remove yourself from the source of heat. Take a break.

Self-induced pressure

Some swimmers push themselves harder than any coach or parent could. Coaches and parents need to be understanding and supportive rather than adding to the tension a swimmer may already be applying to himself. A child

Motivation

Factors that aid motivation:
• receiving encouragement and/or recognition from others;
• having a competitive nature;
• desiring and/or experiencing success;
• enjoying the sport, physically and emotionally;
• enjoying being part of the team.

Factors that hinder motivation:
• a negative attitude;
• anxiety about practice, competition, or those you are interacting with;
• lack of support from adults and/or peers;
• distractions or other activities that get in the way of being able to focus or commit fully;
• goals set too high and a repeated sense of failure;
• burnout.

needs encouragement from adults, especially in competitive situations where he or she may meet failure as well as success. You can say, there is no such thing as failure, for improvement (of times, techniques, and race strategies) is the goal. Yet there are moments when a swimmer races and doesn't place as he or she expected. The athlete may have worked hard, thought he or she should have done better, and thus is disappointed. You can expound any theory on failure that you want; this doesn't change how the child feels when he or she climbs out of the pool, even when knowing improvement has taken place. A child may have conflicting emotions, may pretend not to care about something when in reality he or she cares a lot. Coach and swimmer should sort out the reasons for any disappointments, reassess goals, and discuss what can be changed to have a better chance of reaching an adjusted goal next time.

Swimmers come and go

Swimmers drop out for various reasons. As children grow older, they determine which activities they most enjoy and which activities they are best at and then choose one interest over another. Interests change with age, and trying out various sports when young can be a good thing. This is part of being a well-rounded person. Also, as children get older, being with friends may become a priority in their lives. If their friends aren't swimming, they might drop out.

No matter how good a job a coach does, a swimmer may quit at the height of his or her ability, at the peak of a season, or in the middle of a meet. Normally, these extremes do not occur, but if they do, you must let go. Don't take your swimmers' comings and goings personally. Focus on the students you have, regardless of whether they are going to be around next season, for there are no guarantees. If you let a swimmer go, the experience remains positive. You leave the door open for the swimmer to feel that he or she can return.

Behavior

As a group, children can be wild. They may not listen well, especially the youngest ones. When you tell a child "no," he or she may continue to misbehave. Children test you to see where your limits and their boundaries are. Problems should be dealt with promptly to keep them from developing out of proportion. Talking to a child (or parent) before or after practice is less disruptive and better for the team. If you have to talk to a child during practice, pull him or her aside and talk away from other swimmers. If a child misbehaves repeatedly, if you have talked to him or her several times and there is no change, call the parents. Arrange a conference, so you, the parent, and the child can be present. Allow all parties to express their thoughts and feelings.

Some swimmers will save confrontations with their peers for the moment when they are out of range of their coach. A misbehavior unseen cannot be proved. For example, one swimmer tattles on another. The second swimmer denies that he or she did anything wrong. The second swimmer may even state that the first swimmer started it. How can you reprimand anyone when both views contradict? You can try to get other opinions, building a minor complaint into a major one, or you can nip the problem at the start and lecture both children. To spend time on small problems is a tremendous waste of energy and affects the morale and performance of the team.

Resistance: You expect children who participate on a team to cooperate, but you sometimes meet resistance. One child's resistance must be dealt with, because it can spread like a virus, causing others on the team to join in and side with their peers. Those who don't join in are still affected by it. One uncooperative individual can leave, for resistance is always disruptive and slows down a practice. Those who want to follow the program, which was designed with their best interests in mind, can stay.

Excuses: When coaching, you hear numerous excuses. I forgot my suit; I lost my goggles; my goggles broke; I can't swim without goggles; my father won't let me do the butterfly. "My shoulder hurts" or "I don't feel well" are excuses that you can't ignore, for they may be true. This swimmer should call the parent and leave for the day. If a swimmer cuts practice short due to an untrue excuse, he or she will miss out on learning more and becoming better.

In conclusion: The coach needs to let swimmers know what the rules and expectations are. When rules are broken, when expectations are not met, the coach needs to confront the swimmer immediately, and be clear and specific about what the problem is. All swimmers should be treated equally and that includes disciplining one child the same way as another.

Competitive values

A coach should teach age-group swimmers certain competitive values—respect for one another, the coach, those from opposing teams; the spirit of fair play and the importance of being a good sport; discipline.

Respect for others: You may question whether this is a necessary ingredient to success. While there is an individual aspect to swimming, there is also the team to consider. A swimmer does not exist in a vacuum—especially young swimmers, who are in the process of learning from their coach and their teammates. Not to open yourself up to other swimmers hinders the learning.

Sportsmanship: In competition, a good sport controls negative feelings. He or she smiles and congratulates the winner when defeated and refuses to boast when in the lead. He is friendly to his opponents and enjoys the challenge of competition.

The worker (case study #12)

Amber sets high goals for herself every season and attends practice prepared to give her all. She pushes hard, usually accomplishes her goals, although at the end of each season she inevitably loses steam—and enthusiasm.

Amber joined the team at age six. At age eight, she swam as a ten-and-under and broke pool records with AAA times. At age nine and ten, she continued to improve her times and was AAA in every event. Season after season, she has made the most points for the team. She walks away from all meets with at least one blue ribbon. The others on the team, regardless of age, look up to her—and also expect her to win.

As Amber's coach, you need to keep an eye on how much her teammates expect of her and how much she expects of herself. At the end of the season, when she is losing momentum, remind her of her goals and help her to target them; then give her some time off.

The dogger (case study #13)

Kimberly starts off the season with enthusiasm and a desire to work. She never gives one-hundred percent, but as she matures over the years, she gives more—and slowly chips seconds off her time. If she sticks with the sport, she could excel should her commitment level change. But she will not experience immediate success, because she is not willing to practice hard. She enjoys the social aspects of swim team.

When she starts to hurt in practice, she misbehaves. She stops at the wall or moves out of her lane, talks to or splashes someone next to her. One day she moves to the deep end and you ask her what she is doing.

She says, "I want to practice turns in the deep end."

You tell her, "We are not working on that now," and she begs you to let her do this anyway.

Meanwhile the other non-workers on the team start to drift over. You send them all back to their lanes. She has succeeded in distracting quite a few swimmers.

This same child who dogs practice is different at a meet; she is one-hundred percent focused and cooperative and swims her hardest. When she sees improvement, she runs up to you and says, "I beat my time!"

This swimmer does not understand the relationship between working hard and doing well. Think what she could do if she applied full effort.

The confused swimmer (case study #14)

One day Laurie wants to quit the team and the next day she loves it and wants to continue. When she comes home, wanting to quit, her mother wants to know why, so Laurie creates excuses of things wrong with the team (other children, the coach) rather than admitting that her desire to quit comes from within. She is thirteen, has been swimming competitively for four years, and has not been experiencing much success lately. She realizes that she has to work a lot harder at this point in her swimming career to succeed, and she is not sure she wants to. Her parents are involved in the club and enthusiastic about her participation. Laurie is afraid to admit the truth to her parents, because she believes they will be disappointed.

Finally, the mother tells Laurie she must decide one way or the other—to stay on the team or quit—and that whatever she decides there's no turning back. Laurie quits in the middle of the season, two days before a championship. Laurie is scheduled to swim a relay and a replacement can't be found at the last minute; thus, the other three girls on the relay team cannot swim the event. Meanwhile, the coach is shocked, had no idea Laurie was that unhappy, and wondered how he could have been that out of touch with her not to have known.

If the coach, parent, and swimmer in this situation had been communicating properly, they could have worked together for a better resolution. Laurie could have dealt with her confusion better if she could have been open with the adults in her life. The parent should have made the child follow through on her commitment to the team before dropping out and also talked to the coach, letting him know there was a problem and giving him a chance to be part of the solution. And the coach should have been on the alert, noticing signals of dissatisfaction in his or her swimmers.

Once you notice a problem with a swimmer, determine the source. Are the goals set too high? Lowering expectations may relieve the anxiety. Perhaps the confusion stems from having three choices—to be involved halfway, all the way, or not at all. The swimmer knows he or she could give more and do better, but giving more means sacrificing other things of equal importance. Maybe other activities in the swimmer's life conflict with practice times or meet days. Is a parent, the coach, or a teammate causing the stress? That needs to be resolved in order for the swimmer to continue.

The half-committed swimmer (case study #15)

Jake joins the team, but attends practice sporadically. The coach overlooks this because Jake is a good swimmer and scores points for the team. The team is small, competes against larger town teams, and needs all the points it can get (so the coach believes). The coach encourages Jake to attend practice more, but doesn't require his attendance. Jake finishes the season, but does not return the following school year.

Later, the coach runs into Jake's parent who says, "Jake quit because someone stole money from him in the locker room, and when he told you, you didn't do anything."

Meanwhile, the coach believes that Jake did not inform him of the theft, for he would have done something about it.

The coach, in this situation, is asking for problems in allowing one swimmer to attend practice whenever he or she feels like it. Other swimmers will follow suit, and you will have a team of half-committed swimmers. Being on the team should be a privilege that one needs to maintain by working hard. As far as which team gets the most points in a meet, a coach's focus should be on training swimmers adequately. Often, parents judge a coach by whether the team wins or loses, which may pressure a coach to hang on to talented, but also half-committed swimmers.

Next, the coach should encourage open communication with all swimmers and parents. The coach should try to sense a problem that a swimmer may be feeling and not expressing and ask if something is wrong. If you get to know your swimmers and how they react to things, you should be able to tell if there is a problem. If Jake did not report the theft to the coach, he used this as an excuse to quit the team, a team he was obviously only partially interested in to begin with. Many children (and adults) do not want to take responsibility for their own actions. It is someone else's fault, not their own. Children who are pressured by adults to stay on a team may use any excuse to quit.

The last possibility is that Jake did report the incident to the coach, and the coach did not hear him, or was not paying attention. A tremendous amount of stimuli are coming at the coach in one practice—many children and many parents have questions to ask or comments to make. The noise level in the pool area is usually high. A child may tell the coach something when he or she is obviously busy or involved with something else. The best the coach can do in this situation is to try to be as alert as possible to a swimmer's needs. And swimmers and parents need to give a coach a chance to respond. Communication is three-way, and everyone must be equally committed to one another to achieve success.

The Team

What is a team and why team up?

Individuals make up a team; each individual should have a role and be made to feel an important part of the whole. People team up to accomplish something; some common interest brings them together. Learning is expedited in a group setting with a teacher and other students who earnestly pursue the same knowledge. Sharing something you enjoy will enhance your experience. We can usually accomplish more together than alone. When a team clicks, it is magical and inspiring for all those involved. The interaction between the swimmers and the coach makes each season what it is. Each year, the group changes and so do the dynamics.

A team motivates those who are training. A team comes with a coach who, no matter how motivated the swimmer may already be, provides more motivation, gives him or her a direction, as well as tips on how to refine skills. A coach stands outside of a swimmer, looking in, and provides him or her with a different perspective. A student needs to be able to gather objectivity from someone who is an expert in the field.

We learn not only from coaches, but also from teammates. Young or new swimmers learn from watching older, more experienced swimmers, and an older swimmer will learn from his or her peers as well as by assisting a coach. The coach will still be developing the older swimmer, for teaching reinforces learning or makes you think harder about what you know. Often an older swimmer will help a younger, less experienced one without being asked. But a coach can also get a feel for which older swimmers like to help the younger ones and then rely specifically on them. "Andre, can you take Peter over to the deep end and show him the front-flip turn since he missed the demonstration and practice yesterday?" Also, partner a younger swimmer with an older swimmer at a meet; the older swimmer can give the younger swimmer support when the coach is busy.

Through being on a team, the individual improves as long as teammates are positive and supportive of one another, as long as the coach is supportive of the team and the team is supportive of the coach. When everyone works well together, a bond can result. If a swimmer has a strong bond with a team, he or she is more apt to show up for practice and work hard—because he or she wants to be part of that group and feels a loyalty or a commitment to others that compensates for how he or she feels about going to practice that day. The swimmer attends, because others are depending on him or her.

Team spirit

Does a swimmer need team spirit to swim well? Swimming can be perceived as both an individual and team sport. Whether team spirit is essential for a good swim depends on the individual. Team spirit may be important to some individuals (especially young beginners), drawing them to the sport and enabling them to stick with it. Swimming is fun, and friends are there, at the pool. People care about each other; swimmers are part of a family. Others are motivated from within and will push themselves whether the energy outside of them is positive or negative. They won't be affected by the presence or lack of team spirit, because they are determined to attain their goal and will strive despite confrontation, despite the odds.

Team spirit is an attitude. State of mind can make a difference in the training process. Feeling good about what you are doing spreads to others on the team. A positive attitude is infectious, as is a negative one. It is the coach's responsibility to have a positive attitude and to pull up those around him or her. A positive attitude elevates the team, so that everyone does their best—because the team is fun, because they care, and because people on the team care about them.

Team spirit is also commitment. When a group of people commit to excellence, the energy level is high. When the energy level of a group is high, individuals are motivated to reach beyond themselves, to take the next step, and to grow. In sharing that growth, they share a special moment in time they are not likely to forget. Likewise, if some people on a team do not apply full effort, the group is affected.

Team spirit means working together. If individuals are at odds or pursuing their own interests in conflict with team interests, then the group will lack unity. Each individual on a team should accept others and be accepted. Swimmers should support and encourage one another, should try to get along, even if that means tolerating another teammate who is irritating. Coaches should discourage negative remarks and gossip, as they are bad for team moral. Keep negative comments confidential, for spreading them to another, who may spread them to another, leads to distortion. Coaches should also encourage friendships between teammates. Swimming is social as well as personal. Young people make friends both in the water and after practice. They may stay at the pool to play Shark or Marco Polo or cards on the deck.

Swimming as a team (case study #16)

My swimmers were attending USA Swimming sanctioned A, AA, and AAA meets. I had to divide my small team of thirty-five swimmers into different meets. I never had the entire team going to one meet. At these A, AA, AAA meets, team score was rarely calculated. The focus was on the individual performance. The purpose of the team was only to provide the learning atmosphere, but not to be a united front on meet day. Without a team focus at the meets, the team I coached lacked cohesion. Individuals swam for themselves with no loyalty to their teammates. If they were scheduled for a relay team and then missed the meet at the last minute, their attitude was "big deal."

I compared this to teams I grew up on, teams that participated as a team for team points. One team won, one team lost, and all teams gave the meet their best shot. We were taught how to win and how to lose, that all of us experience both at various times in our lives—and we were all in this together. Not only were our own successes and failures considered, but so were our teammates'; neither was more or less important. For most of us children, winning was not the important thing, but swimming and being part of the team was.

When team score is calculated, each swimmer's participation is crucial and the team becomes more important. You can win or lose by a few points, and you can win a lot of points with relay teams alone; thus, full participation is the only condition that can accurately determine a team's potential. With this in mind, I found a dual-meet league for my team to participate in, which did bring our team together.

Swimming without a team (case study #17)

Jack swam competitively on a team as a youngster. Then he moved to a small town that had a pool but no team. He practiced just as often as he had when he was on a team and pursued swimming tips through swim books, magazines, and videos. He wanted to keep competing, so he joined USA Swimming and entered meets unattached, meaning not affiliated with any team. Without a coach and other swimmers to push him in practice, he had to rely on the clock. Because he was an older swimmer with a swimming background and because he was determined, Jack did well, despite the obstacle of working out alone.

Melissa grew up in a small town in Montana, where there was a twenty-five-yard pool. She was interested in swimming, but the pool did not have a team. Her mother encouraged her and then became her coach. Melissa joined USA Swimming, as an unattached swimmer, and was able to participate in individual events. She enjoyed the sport, despite her isolation during workouts. The question for her was to swim or not to swim. When Melissa went to college, she was finally able to compete on a team and experience the camaraderie she had missed in her youth.

A swimmer can swim without a team, but only if he or she is really determined to do so. The young, inexperienced child needs a leader, would not know what direction to go in without a teacher. An older swimmer can continue to train without a coach if he or she has previous swim team experience and knows how to train. Once a swimmer gets older, he or she will benefit from learning how to operate without a coach.

Team success

What makes one team have the edge over another? A successful swim team depends on the community, the group of people involved, the facility, and the policies of that facility. A successful swim team takes a caring coach. If one coach leaves, is there another to take his or her place, to keep the team moving forward? If a coach works hard, the team improves from season to season. After many seasons with a strong coach, you have a strong team.

The age of the team matters. How long has the team been in existence with a strong coach, a strong aquatic program, with the support of a parents' group? This takes effort year after year. As coaches and swimmers come and go, do others step in to keep the program going? If the team continues to progress year after year because of continued support, it will gain its edge.

The more swimmers you have on the team who are older, but started young, the stronger the team. One fast swimmer on a team will push the others. Like a game of dominoes, the faster more swimmers become, the faster the team. Children are competitive and will push to keep up with the person beside them.

Success depends on the region and population density (city, suburb, country). Larger areas have more children to draw upon. The quality, frequency, and intensity of the training are important. How hard do the swimmers work? Is the team able to practice all year round?

The Parents

Invite parents to participate

A successful swim program depends on many jobs getting done. These jobs, which parents can help with, include: recruiting swimmers, ordering supplies, collecting money, banking, keeping records, writing a monthly newsletter, planning and participating in home meets, arranging car pools to away meets, advertising events, reporting meet results, generating sponsors, hosting fund-raisers, organizing an annual awards banquet, and updating a team record board. Many parents have no idea of all the work that goes on behind the scenes. They assume that these tasks are part of the coach's job and that he or she is paid, but this becomes a problem if the coach is not paid enough or at all for these extras. Thus, the coach must educate parents on when and how to help. Allow parents to become part of the team.

If you do not have an organized parent support group, call the parents of your swimmers together and set monthly meetings for the season. Place a time limit on parent meetings. Present an agenda and stick to it. Parents will be more inclined to attend if they know what to expect and how long it will take.

By starting a swim association you have a chance to communicate with parents on a regular basis, and they have more of an investment in the program because they are involved in the decision making. A swim association supports the coach, acts as a buffer when conflict occurs, and creates a power base in the community. Parents can form a non-profit organization by filing a master business application, electing officers, writing by-laws, and setting monthly meetings. Dues, contributions from civic organizations, and fund-raising activities finance a non-profit organization.

Keep parents informed

Handouts given to children to take home will save you the expense of mailing, but do not always reach the parents. If you want the parents to be well-informed, and they are not attending the pool on a regular basis, mail them a monthly newsletter. Yet even then, some parents do not read information mailed to them.

The solution: The newsletter should be one of many ways in which you relay important information to the parents. Other ways include: informing your swimmers at practice and asking them to tell their parents; holding monthly parent meetings; calling parents when they do not respond to an important deadline that you addressed in a newsletter or at a meeting; posting news (and deadlines) on a bulletin board at the pool; establishing a phone tree, a link from one parent to the next, as a way to relay sudden news, such as the cancellation of a meet.

A booklet, handed out on registration day, lets parents know important team dates and times, as well as what the seasonal costs will be for their child to participate. Costs include USA

Swimming membership fee, meet fees, and travel expenses; suits, cap, goggles, and towel; and dues per month. Parents typically pay monthly dues to the team their child joins; dues vary from team to team and season to season.

Parental involvement

Parents get involved in different ways. Some parents want to be involved in every aspect of their child's life. This is good, as long as they keep a positive outlook rather than trying to pick apart everything a child or coach does. Yet some parents don't know when to let go and allow their children to enjoy an experience without constant interference. The absent parent presents an opposite extreme. This parent never attends practices or meets, has no idea what is going on or who their child is with. This is sad for the child.

Of course, the ideal lies between these two extremes. The parent drops the child at practice and returns at the end. He or she can catch the last few minutes of practice and while waiting for the child to dress can get to know the coach and other parents. When parents are absent from practice, but not from meets, more gets accomplished, because you have one less factor to equate.

Turn interference into something positive (case study #18)

An aggressive mother attends every practice and takes up your time before, after, and sometimes during practice. She believes that because her daughter excels in everything she does and shows a natural talent for swimming, she should get extra attention. Be firm with this parent in letting her know that yes, her daughter is special, but only one of many on a team and that every individual needs to be considered.

Also, do not allow parents on the deck during practice. Parents may volunteer to help with practice, and if you let them, they almost always get in the way. When you are on the deck, your focus needs to be on the swimmers, not on the parents. Many swimmers need attention, and every second counts. Parents aren't trained coaches, and you don't have time to train them.

Encourage this mother to get involved, direct her energy, give her a specific job. In this way, you can turn her interference, which is negative, into involvement, which is positive—positive not only for her, but also for her child and for everyone else on the team.

Educate parents (case study #19)

One day at practice, a parent walked up to the poolside, with a smile on her face, and said to her child, "Show me what you're practicing," and the young girl began to swim the backstroke. The parent told the child to cup her hands, so that she could push the water better. The coach, horrified, looked at the parent and said to both her and the child, "No! You don't want to do that. You want the fingers to be loose, not squeezed together tightly. The hand should be natural."

Some parents think they know something when they really don't. This is often the case with parents who were competitive swimmers when they were younger and now want to be a coach to their child. The problem with this is that swimming is an evolving sport and most of the swimmers who were coached in the sixties, seventies, and even eighties execute movements that are outdated, unless they have kept up with the sport.

In this case, politely remind the parent of the rule: no one but swimmers are allowed on the deck. Also while you are there to educate your swimmers, swimmers come with parents who often need to be educated too. If a parent is talking about stroke mechanics in front of you and is wrong, make the correction. The more the parents know, the better.

Parental Pressure

Parents can be supportive and helpful or they can be demanding and negative. You need parents behind you, although they are not always behind you in the way you may want. Often you have to grin and bear the inefficiencies and get along with everyone for the sake of the team.

A coach must be sensitive to the children's needs, but wear a shield of armor when dealing with negative adult energy. If parents are unsupportive of a coach, you have a bad situation. Every problem can be solved, but people have to be willing to work together—and parents, athletes, and coach should work together. Thus, while factoring parents in can complicate a coach's job, there is no way around it. Not only do you have to deal with parents, but in order to be effective you need to have the majority of the parents on your side. Generally, if the children like you, the parents will like you. Nonetheless, parents can be a big source of stress.

Pressure from a parent is not in the swimmer's best interest, nor is it in the coach's or team's best interest. Parents should offer the child encouragement and trust the coach, who is the swimming expert. Yet no matter how knowledgeable, well-qualified, and professional you are and how much you put into the job, it will never be enough for some parents. It is human nature for people to criticize and be dissatisfied.

Usually for every non-supportive parent there is a supportive one. Find your supportive parents and communicate regularly with them. Educate them, so they are an asset. Often it is ignorance that leads to doubt. The supportive parents can serve as a buffer, sheltering you from those forces that hinder progress. Remember that negativity is an attitude, and attitudes can be changed. This takes effort on the part of the coach--to communicate and to try to understand the parent's perspective. Talk to the parents, get to know them. Don't have a distant or silent relationship. If you see the parents on the bleachers, watching from afar, walk over and talk to them.

No one is perfect. Every coach has one or two regrets, a disappointing experience, a hurtful relationship with a child or parent, a situation that didn't go the right way. If there is a communication breakdown, perhaps you could have been clearer and prevented the problem. Try to analyze what happened and learn by the mistakes rather than repeat them. You cannot erase mistakes and oftentimes cannot make amends. All you can do is your best. If that falls short of other people's expectations, you cannot blame yourself. Look ahead, not back. Focus on coaching well and taking your swimmers and team as far as you can. You will never make one-hundred percent of the parents happy. That job is impossible, so don't even try.

Expectations (case study #20)

Evan joins the swim team, participates in his first meet, and doesn't place. His father blames the coach for not teaching him well enough, but the coach taught Evan as well as he could for the time he had to work with him. Development in a swimmer takes time. A beginning swim teamer can catch up with others in his or her age group who have been swimming harder for longer, but not overnight. Some parents don't understand this and just want to see their child win. If their child doesn't win, someone is at fault—whereas the true fault is on the focus.

When a swimmer is in his or her first season, with so much yet to learn, the focus should not be on winning, but rather on learning. Beginning swim teamers attend B and A meets, where they can experience success and be encouraged to continue to strive to improve. As experience and ability grow, they move up, to AA and AAA meets. Thus, swimmers are always competing against others who are similar in speed. Breaking out of A into AA times or out of AA into AAA times is more of an accomplishment for a young swimmer than winning or losing a race, for this is a true sign of improvement.

Parents should not criticize the child's performance, nor should they tell a disappointed swimmer "great job," for that will come across as phony and out of touch with his or her feelings. Parents must give the child space to breathe and the freedom to feel the way he or she does. Sometimes competitive situations can be too tense. Adults become too serious and forget that the object is to learn, to improve, and have fun. The pressure to win for young swimmers—who are in the process of learning—can be frustrating. If competition becomes too negative, a child may be turned off from the sport completely. Children can be turned off in numerous ways and that is what we are trying to avoid. You need to cut down on external pressure and let them decide to come and go for themselves.

Communication breakdown (case study #21)
The last day of school before Christmas break is a half-day, and you call an optional practice. High-school swimmers finish school at noon, and junior-high students finish at one p.m. Laurel is in the junior high and comes to the pool (which is on school grounds) at 11:45 a.m., her lunch hour, and tells you that her parents gave permission for her to get out of school one hour early to swim with the high-school students, which is the group she usually swims with after a regular school day. She tells you that someone has to sign her out and asks you to come to the office with her.

You walk with Laurel to the school office, which is in the next building, and the secretary informs you that Laurel has to have parental permission. Laurel say, "My parents said it was okay."

"I need a note from them," the secretary replies.

"They are home. Can you call them?" Laurel asks.

The secretary calls the parents, who consent but comment, " Next time the coach should tell us when there is an extra practice."

You are upset, because the practice is optional. You cannot call every parent who doesn't come to the pool to tell them about an optional practice. The swimmer has to show some responsibility. The swimmer told you that her parents knew about the practice, yet the parents did not know and heard about it for the first time from the secretary. If you had known the truth, you would have never have gone to the office to sign Laurel out. She did not have to attend the optional practice at noon. She could have come at one p.m.

PART THREE

Personal Equipment

Suits

A swimmer should have a practice suit and a team suit. While a heavyweight suit is fine for workouts, the thinnest suit possible is best for meets. A thin suit creates less friction drag than a thick suit, and the less drag, the faster the swimmer. Also, because of their thinness, Lycra racing suits wear out quickly when worn on a daily basis.

Caps

Swimmers wear caps for two reasons: to move faster through the water and to protect their hair. Try swimming with a thin cap for a week; then swim without it. You will notice a difference—you will feel slower without the cap.

The thinner the cap, the less resistance, the faster the swimmer. Yet there is a time and place for thicker caps. A cap holds in heat and keeps the swimmer warm in cool water. Silicone caps work especially well for open water swimming. But in a warm pool, a thin cap works best—not only to reduce friction drag, but also to prevent the swimmer from overheating and tiring faster.

Some swimmers are concerned about the effects of chlorine on their hair. A cap offers a lot of protection. In addition, swimmers can use shampoo, cream rinse, and protein conditioners or can apply a leave-in conditioner to the ends (the most vulnerable part) of the hair before putting the cap on. Chlorine coats the hair and then drips down and collects on the ends, which become bleached. Frequent exposure to chlorine may make hair look thin, but does not create hair loss. While ends may be damaged, hair can be trimmed; thus, swimming does not permanently damage hair.

Goggles

A swimmer needs goggles to swim for any length of time in most swimming pools (especially indoor). Children will attend practice without goggles, and when their eyes start to burn, they become distracted.

There are several reasons why children attend practice without goggles: 1) They may not have been given any to begin with. Their parents (non-swimmers) may not understand the importance of the investment; sometimes parents can be overwhelmed with all the material things their children say they need. 2) Or the parents may realize the importance, but haven't gotten around to buying the goggles yet. 3) More often, parents buy their children goggles, and children leave them at home or lose them. Parents, often in a state of frustration, buy a second pair. When the second pair is lost, children do not want to tell their parents (especially if the second pair was only a week old), so they attend practice, willing to bear the pain—or hoping to borrow from you.

55

And if out of sympathy you lend your own, you can't count on getting them back. A coach who lends goggles will often reach into his or her bag at workout time and find none. This situation can be overwhelming, as you will have half your team asking for suits, caps, or goggles, because they forgot theirs. It is best right from the start to establish a rule that if they do not have a suit, cap, or goggles, they cannot work out that day. Sharing goggles, even though they have been immersed in chlorine, is unhealthy and does not teach the child responsibility. Each child should have his or her own goggles and learn to take care of them. Part of being a serious swimmer is owning and learning to care for your own equipment. Inform parents of the importance of goggles. This is one item they cannot cut corners on and buy tomorrow. The children need the goggles on the first day of practice and on all other days as well. It should be the parent's responsibility, not the coach's, to make sure the child has goggles and remembers to bring them daily.

Since children (especially those twelve-and-under) easily lose goggles, it is helpful for the parents to write their name on the strap. If the goggles are left on the deck, the coach or lifeguard will pick them up, see the name, and be able to return them. For working out, I recommend anti-fog goggles with a plastic rather than foam seal, as the foam-sealed goggles leak. Eventually, over time, all goggles will get scratched and start to fog. You can buy replaceable straps and rims, but when the lens wear out, you might as well use them for awhile as a spare and then toss them.

Case study #22

Patsy is ten years old and a good swimmer. On this particular day, she swims in a lane with five other swimmers of similar speed. There are approximately twenty-five children in the pool and two coaches on deck. The team-policy booklet, sent home with parents on registration day, states that goggles are "recommended." The booklet states that the chlorine in the pool is strong, that children swimming without goggles will be in pain and will return home with red eyes. The booklet also states that the pool does not supply goggles, because handing out the same pair over and over to many different children is a possible health hazard. Those who argue say disease transmission is impossible because of the chlorine in the pool. This does not change the fact that the pool cannot afford to supply goggles for each child.

Patsy often attends practice without goggles. Her parents do not attend the workouts, only the meets, and assume that the goggles they bought for her originally are still with her; she hasn't told them differently. On this particular day, she is swimming butterfly with her eyes closed and runs into the wall, chipping her front tooth. The parents take her to the dentist to have the tooth capped and then mail the bill to the Recreation Department; the Department administrators refuse to pay. The parents then take the matter to court and win. Patsy's father believes that the pool should supply goggles for all of the swimmers. He says the goggles can be dropped into a bucket at the end of each workout to be picked up at the beginning of the next—and sterilized between uses. The result of this conflict: the swim-team booklet is changed to goggles "required" rather than "recommended."

Practice

Expectations

Swimmers should be told ahead of time what to expect in practice. You can do this by meeting with the group at the beginning of a season and also by gathering briefly before or after practice. Instill a sense of urgency in your swimmers, so they come to practice prepared to work. Stress the importance of giving one-hundred percent during practice. In order to become competent swimmers, they must commit to the learning process. Make it clear from the beginning what they are committing to, and do not give them the option of withdrawing mid-season. Ask parents for their support in this. Swimmers cannot realize their potential in the sport without making a commitment. Also, a team cannot be a team unless all of its members commit.

Organizing practices

Plan practices ahead of time and then stay on track. This makes for organized workouts, meaning more learning will occur. Planning well means utilizing pool space and time to the fullest. For example, if you have more swimmers than you can fit into lanes, divide the group into separate time slots. Avoid overcrowding lanes, if possible. It's hard to have a good workout when people are bumping into each other.

Once the plan is in place and the season has begun, be sure to arrive early, so that you can set up and settle in before the practice begins. Make sure you have enough of whatever equipment you plan to use that day—such as kickboards, pull buoys, hand paddles, and ankle bands. Check for broken straps, sharp edges, loose ends. Position the equipment for easy access (for both

you and the swimmers). Write the workout on a board that is visible to all swimmers. Scope out the pool area for any last minute details. Perhaps while planning at home, there is something that you forgot that being at the pool early will help you remember. Then relax for a few minutes, so that you can begin each practice refreshed, rather than frazzled.

Practices should start and end on time. Do not change times or dates unless necessary. Your athletes need a routine to follow, and you want to minimize confusion. While establishing a swimming routine is important when training and striving to improve, varying daily workouts will make time in the pool more interesting, which also means that swimmers will tune in and thus learn more.

In the beginning of the season, varying workouts is especially easy, because there is so much to teach—and learn. Your swimmers must learn adequate strokes, turns, and starts—or refine what they know. You can use drills (and there are so many of them) to teach important concepts. Keep your athletes moving and busy learning new things, so that they feel challenged, but with skills they can accomplish. Experiment with new techniques and training methods; this will add interest to the workout—for both you and the swimmers.

Whatever your plan, adapt the lesson to the group you are teaching. The same group of children can vary in mood and behavior daily. If practice needs a change of direction, because your swimmers don't respond that day to the plan, have alternatives. When tensions are high, incorporate fun into the workout. Your eight-and-under team will need fun activities to stay motivated. Older swimmers who feel pressured to do well by parents, peers, or self need a coach to lift them up. It is important for swimmers to know their coach on a fun level, not just as someone who is always pushing them to do something they may or may not want to do. If you play deck and water games with them occasionally, they will not only see you as a coach, but also as a person to have fun with, to relate to, and to feel comfortable with.

As the cliche goes, "All work and no play" can be stagnating for a young athlete. If an athlete grows bored with a sport, chances are he or she will quit. If the athlete quits before feeling some degree of success, he or she may never return to the sport. If a young athlete has a positive experience—where work is involved, but so is fun, and where progress is made—you give him or her something to stick with or return to.

Reading and writing workouts

Collect workouts and assemble them in a notebook. Label them early season, mid-season, and late season. Note workouts that went well—with which age groups and at what point in the season. You may even want to take into account what day of the week it was, or other special circumstances, such as holidays. What works and what doesn't depends on the group of swimmers and depends on how the coach implements it. Do all this pre-season, in the planning phase.

While reading workout books can give you good ideas, it is also important to be creative and write your own workouts. You need to challenge yourself as well as your swimmers, and only you know your team and the type of workout they need. To follow a preset workout written by someone else without your particular group in mind may save time, but will not give you the same results. Thus, while your plan is set prior to the season, you tailor workouts to fit the group once the season begins.

Teach your swimmers what goes into a workout. Thus, if they want to come to the pool during lap swim and work out on their own, they will have many ideas on how to create their own workout. The more you teach them to do on their own, the more confident and proficient they become.

Teach swimmers how to read workouts, and use the same terminology that is used in competition; for example, say "Swim a 100," instead of saying "Swim four laps." Explain to young swimmers that the pool is twenty-five yards long and quiz them: "200 yards equals how many laps?" This is part of their education, and they are quite capable of learning. Also teach swimmers to look at the pace clock. They should know how long it takes to swim fifty yards, and they should be able to time their rests. The younger ones will need a lot of help with this while the older swimmers will do this automatically, if they have been trained properly.

Teaching swimming etiquette

Proper behavior when swimming varies slightly from pool to pool, but is usually universal. Swimmers must be courteous to those in their lane. They must not disrupt another's workout, unless it is an emergency. Lane lines separate one lane from another. Children will try to hang on these lines. Do not let them. Whenever giving a child a "do-not," let them know why: They will stretch out the lines; the lines may break; someone will have to buy new ones, and they are expensive.

The way the coach arranges the swimmers into lane lines will have a big effect on how the workout goes that day. After assigning lanes, the coach lets the workout flow, and if someone seems misplaced, the coach can move him or her, so the workout runs smoothly for everyone. If there are two swimmers in a lane, you can split the lane. If there are three or more, then swimmers circle, always staying to the right of the black (center) line. A coach should group swimmers according to speed, allowing the fastest swimmer to lead. If swimmers are keeping a pace that matches their ability, then they will have a better workout; there will be less slowing down or speeding up. When passing, they pass to the left, in the middle of the lane. The person being passed pulls to the right, close to the lane line, or anticipates the faster swimmer approaching and pauses when at the wall to let him or her pass.

You can organize your swimmers so they swim in waves. If you have six lanes and four swimmers per lane, each swimmer is assigned a number between one and four. You give the swimmers an activity, and then you start the ones, then the twos, then the threes, and finally the fours. When teaching swimmers an important concept, you can increase the send-off time, so that you are able to watch each group more thoroughly.

If you have enough coaches, you can set up stations and rotate swimmers. For example, one coach works on turns in the deep end while another works on starts in one lane; a third coach drills swimmers in the remaining lanes. Swimmers spend equal time at each station, rotating at the sound of a whistle, or any other agreed-upon signal. If swimmers spend fifteen minutes at each station, and you allow a few minutes in-between for rotation, the entire activity involves approximately fifty minutes.

Problem solving

At 3:15 the pool doors open and the children rush in. Young swimmers may have forgotten suits, caps, and goggles and ask to borrow these items, even though you have told them many times that lending is against pool policy. They then call their parents to try to obtain these things, which means they will be late. These children can hold you up, because you are supervising the phone when you should be on deck, starting practice.

You can spend your whole workout answering questions and problem solving, which is why a lifeguard or office person should be employed during swim team practice. If this is not possible, then ask parents to take turns being at practice to problem solve. Be clear that their job is to help the children get into the pool, not to further distract the coach. The parent-helper must stay off the deck and use his or her best judgment in helping the children with their needs.

Talking to your team for five minutes at the beginning of each practice will help, for children can ask questions at this time. You can repeat swim-team policies and procedures: coming to practice on time, being prepared, being responsible for their own gear, not expecting to borrow what they have forgotten. If they forget their suit, cannot swim, and have to sit on the bleachers and watch for a day, they will be more apt to remember next time.

Swimmers may argue with a coach about the workout or the lane in which they are swimming. Rules that are good to establish regarding practice: 1) Do not argue with the coach. 2) Do not question the workout. Do not ask for free time. The coach planned the workout with a specific purpose in mind. 3) Think of your lane assignment as your lane assignment, not as your lane. You do not possess this lane each time; you cannot form a favorite spot. You may have to move around; it's good to swim in a variety of spots.

Why swimmers stop

I have seen coaches get caught at one side of the pool, where the workout is written. This gives swimmers many reasons to stop. They stop to ask the coach questions about a workout they already understand. They stop to ask the coach to fix their goggles. They stop to tattle on another swimmer. They stop to complain about a shoulder pain or cramp or a headache. They stop to ask when the next meet is. Anything to stop.

Often this is done for attention. Many swimmers want to be recognized, want to be part of your life. They are usually so anxious that they don't give you a chance to reach them before they reach you. Adjusting their goggles five times may just be an excuse to make contact. And sometimes swimmers are tired, hurting, and want to get out of a set. While the coach is diverted by one swimmer, others fool around, loaf, or cheat on their workout.

The solution: The coach should move around the deck and not get bogged down with questions or fixing children's goggles. Keep the swimmers busy, the workout moving. Explain to the swimmers that you care about them all, but you need to keep the workout on track, and questions should be asked before or after, not during practice. Teach swimmers how to fix their own goggles. Sit them down as a group and teach this as you would teach any swimming skill in the pool; it is important for them to learn to do as much as possible on their own.

Safety

Safety should be a coach's primary concern during practice. A coach should educate swimmers on proper behavior; many accidents result from carelessness, irresponsibility, or a lack of knowledge. Focus on preventing accidents before they occur by making sure that swim teamers are educated on how to be safe in and around a swimming pool, are following the rules (such as walking rather than running), and are not partaking in dangerous activities (such as back flips off the side of the pool). Be courteous, but firm about what the rules are and why they must be followed, and make no exceptions. Do not let a swimmer change your position or do something that may be unsafe. Making exceptions will only confuse people—especially children.

A safe facility

Provide a safe environment for your swimmers. Monitor water and air temperature. For example, if the water is too warm and you are working your swimmers hard, they may get overheated, exhausted, and even ill. Also, monitor the chemical balance in the water by taking readings for chlorine and ph several times daily. The water should also be clear; the pool should be vacuumed and backwashed regularly. If the water is unsafe, do not let swimmers in.

Make sure that the deck is clear, that nothing has been left lying around that someone could trip over. Hazardous areas at a pool should be corrected, if possible, or marked and supervised. Make swimmers aware of potential hazards in and around the pool. The entrance and exit areas may be slippery, because they are heavily traveled by wet people. Also, people may collide with one another. Broken tiles with sharp edges where swimmers may easily cut a hand or foot must be fixed as soon as possible and marked until fixed.

A locker room is often unsupervised and becomes a place to misbehave, which can lead to an accident. If you are too busy, ask lifeguards or assistant coaches to routinely check locker rooms, especially at the crucial times when children are arriving and leaving. When parents are around, ask them for help. If you are dealing with large numbers of swimmers, you should have help.

An Emergency Action Plan

Your workplace should have a plan that can be activated if there is an emergency. If an emergency occurs, following a plan is simpler than having to decide what to do on the spot. All employees should be notified of the plan, and it is wise to hold in-service training sessions, so they can practice.

An Emergency Action Plan should be specific in nature. What is the pool's first aid policy for a seizure, bloody nose, or fainting spell? While lifeguards and swim coaches are CPR and First Aid certified, you must assess the criteria and apply it to your specific pool. For example, in the case of a spinal injury, your pool policy may state that you turn the victim face up (as learned from the American Red Cross) and move him or her to the shallow end, where you stabilize the person until the EMTs arrive. For your pool this is realistic and practical, because the fire department is three blocks away and will come with more help and better equipment. For another pool with a fire department farther away, backboarding the victim and getting him or her out of the water may be crucial, so that body temperature can be more easily stabilized and to prevent shock from setting in.

An Emergency Action Plan helps those involved in a rescue to respond as a team rather than with opposing force. There is a plan in place to follow; it is that easy. If a staff member disagrees with a course of action and wants to appeal to his or her boss and co-workers to adust the plan, this must be done prior to, not during an emergency. Thus, the manager, coach, and lifeguard are operating from the same page; this is important, for the safety of the patrons.

Equipment safety

The coach should inspect the equipment daily to make sure it is in working order. Teach swimmers how to use the equipment properly, for misuse may cause injury. Teach them to recognize equipment failure and what to do if something breaks in the middle of a practice. Broken or outdated equipment should be repaired or thrown away. The coach should also make sure that the equipment fits or is adjusted to the swimmer so that it does not restrict movement and cause injury.

Emphasize to your swimmers that equipment is for work, not play. For example, do not let a swimmer submerge a kickboard with his or her hands, or sit or stand on one. If a swimmer loses hold of a submerged kickboard, it will pop out of the water with force and can hit someone. A hard kickboard with a sharp corner that hits someone in the eye may cause a serious injury.

The coach wears a whistle and uses it when starting swimmers, to clear the pool after a swim, in a hazardous situation, when he or she cannot get the attention of a swimmer who is misbehaving, and in an emergency. The children will want to blow your whistle; do not let them. Explain that the whistle is an important piece of equipment, not a toy. And it is not healthy to share whistles, even with co-workers.

Children will also want to use or play with your stop watch. To lend your whistle or stopwatch is a means of losing control. The next thing you know you will have neither, as they dance away and leave these things elsewhere. Like the whistle, a stopwatch is a delicate piece of equipment that you need at all times.

Proper supervision

A certified lifeguard must be on deck during practice. The coach may act as both coach and lifeguard, depending on the number of swimmers practicing. But the coach cannot be expected to supervise any other activities in the pool other than swim team. The coach cannot monitor the front desk, office, or phone and then coach safely and appropriately. All swimmers, no matter how competent they are, must be supervised. Anything can happen at anytime, even to an experienced swimmer.

Don't leave the deck unsupervised when swimmers are in the water. Because your full attention needs to be on the pool, talk to assistants, parents, and patrons before or after practice. Do not answer the phone while coaching. That should be the job of a desk clerk or an answering machine. If you are the only one working at the pool during practice time, let the phone ring. It is up to the administration to staff the pool properly. Let the administration know that cutting corners can result in an unsafe situation. You are liable should an accident occur and negligence be proven. By trying to wear too many hats, you may be placing yourself in a dangerous position. Protect the child and protect yourself. Don't assume that because most swim teamers are good swimmers that an accident can't or won't occur.

Monitoring behavior

Rule #1: Walk rather than run. It often helps when implementing a rule to give the children an answer to "why." The deck is hard (often cement or tile) and can be slippery when wet. If someone slips and falls, especially at the speed of a run, he or she can be hurt.

Rule #2: No pushing, dunking, or splashing. A person who is pushed can slip, fall, hit something hard or sharp, or even collide with someone else swimming by. Dunking may interfere with a person getting a breath. Someone may be in serious trouble under the water before the joker who is doing the dunking even realizes it. In lifeguarding, a course for competent swimmers, a signal (the pinch) is often used should someone under the water suddenly get into trouble. Again, even good swimmers can become victims. Safe behavior prevents accidents. Both dunking and splashing are obnoxious behaviors that interfere with the workout of a swim teamer and should not be allowed.

Rule #3: Don't eat a large meal immediately before working out. Wait an hour after a large meal or twenty minutes after a light snack (a granola bar and orange juice). Children who want a snack after school and before practice may find lightly flavored bottled water an attractive option. Drinking water before a workout is best.

If a swimmer does get a stomach cramp from swimming too soon after eating too much, pull him or her out of the water immediately. The swimmer should stay warm (covered with a towel) while sitting on a bench (or chair), resting and watching the others. Give the child a particular assignment, something specific to watch for, so he or she will be learning even though not swimming. Make sure that the child rests enough (question him or her on how much was eaten when) and is completely recovered before returning to the workout. The child should then be given a light workout and told to avoid eating before practice next time.

Rule #4: Swimmers must not dive into less than five feet of water—without a lot of training and an okay from the coach. Make sure a swimmer has mastered a long shallow dive before diving from a block into the shallow end of some pools (at meets).

At practice, teach racing dives in deep water. Preferably start swimmers in at least nine feet of water and taper swimming depths as the racing dive is mastered. Coaches need to situate starting blocks at the deepest end of the pool, which hopefully will be more than five feet. In addition, swimmers must not be allowed to horseplay on the starting blocks and must make sure that when it is their turn to go that the lane is clear.

Teaching and Learning
Part I

Learning to swim

Children should learn to swim for safety reasons and because swimming offers a lifetime of enjoyment. At a pool, children make friends and are part of many fun activities. They develop positive relationships built on good health. Swimming and health are directly related. Just jumping in the pool, being immersed in water, offers pleasure of the deepest kind.

Children should learn to swim in a structured environment. Lessons are the foundation, a place where children work their way through the swimming levels and know by the completion of Level IV (American Red Cross) whether they enjoy swimming enough to join a team. The local learn-to-swim program is where all future age group swimmers begin. Every coach should be concerned about the quality of the learn-to-swim program in the area where he or she is coaching, for a positive experience and success at that level will more likely lead children to join the team. On a swim team, children learn technique and train for competition. They become better swimmers, and there is pride in that.

Success in swimming is more likely to occur when a child starts training as young as six and definitely by seven or eight, depending on his or her skill level. Starting swim team as an eight-and-under means starting swim lessons as early as possible. The American Red Cross learn-to-swim program encourages parents to enroll their children in lessons at six-months-old (with an adult) or at three-years-old (without an adult). Outside of lessons, exposing a child frequently to water in a safe and supervised and fun environment will encourage learning. A young child can also learn by watching older swimmers. If a child displays enthusiasm and a potential for swimming, parent and child can attend a swim team practice or meet, just to watch.

Swimmers who start as eight-and-unders and swim through high school without any breaks have a higher success rate than swimmers who start late, stop early, and take breaks. There is a big difference between a swimmer who starts swimming at age eleven, still has to master technique and build swimming muscles, and an eleven-year-old who has been training since age seven and hit AAA times at age nine. The beginning eleven-year-old will have a difficult time catching up with the experienced eleven-year-old. A beginning eleven-year-old, if he or she wants success and works hard, can catch up eventually, but realistically not in one or even two seasons. All swimmers need to go through a process of development in both technique and training, and need to understand concepts and apply them before they can even begin to realize their potential.

A coach can help beginners best by helping them understand the developmental process. If beginners can understand where they are within the big picture, where they want to go and how to get there, the chances are greater that they will remain positive, rather than becoming frustrated. It is not that any of the other swimmers are better. Comparing doesn't work. It is just that the swimmer started at point A and is moving to point B. Show them where on this line they are. Point B is becoming the best they can be, and this takes dedication and time.

Division based on commitment

When teaching swimmers, it is helpful to divide them into groups. One method of division is based on commitment. Recreational swim teamers want to be part of the team, and have fun, but do not have high expectations. They want to learn, but do not apply full effort and do not reach full potential. Other swimmers are competitive, and there are degrees of competitiveness.

First find out what your students want or need from the team. If they are competitive and want to be successful, they need to work for it. Success is the outcome of sustained, hard work, not instant halfway efforts. Becoming successful begins with a decision to excel. You'll do whatever it takes to be great. This includes looking for and understanding new information.

Success is a combination of physical and mental conditioning. To attain an elite level, a swimmer must develop coordination (accuracy of motion and perfection of timing), strength, and speed. The swimmer must be able to intellectualize and internalize the technical aspects of each stroke and needs to be motivated to give his or her full effort; he or she must be willing to work hard to get into top shape. The swimmer must also exhibit natural talent.

Age and skill level

You can also break swimmers into age groups, which is how they compete, but age is not always consistent with skill level. Yet there are obvious physical and mental differences between a swimmer of one age and a swimmer of another, especially when you take the two opposite extremes: the seven-year-old and the eighteen-year-old.

The principle of division allows you to place swimmers of similar abilities together and keep the lessons consistent with the high and low range within that specific group. How you group swimmers will have a big impact on how they learn. While a swimmer may progress from one group to the next, the idea is that he or she is always challenged, but never has to work above his or her potential to the point of becoming frustrated.

You can break down the skill levels of your swimmers in various ways. You may choose three categories: beginner, intermediate, and advanced—although you don't want to verbalize it this way to your swimmers. Instead, you can call them Group A, B, and C—or something like Snappers, Dolphins, and Marlins. Dividing a small team into groups of three may be sufficient, while larger and more advanced teams will need more categories, such as beginner, advanced beginner, intermediate, good, excellent, and elite.

The beginner: Begin with the swimmer's current skill level, and build from there. Build a foundation by teaching proper stroke mechanics. Swimmers at this level easily tire, so allow time for rest, and work on general conditioning principles aimed at building endurance. Incorporate a certain amount of fun into the workout to hold their interest. Games that build endurance are perfect.

Intermediate: Sharpen skills and refine strokes. Break each stroke into parts and use drills. Workouts move from low to moderate, but must still contain some fun. Swimmers at this level have put a certain amount of time and effort into the sport and need some external reward—recognition and encouragement from a coach—to make them feel the increased workload is worth their while.

Advanced: Workouts must be more intense, must be challenging, must push them so that they can meet the demands of competition. If the workout is not hard enough, they will complain; if the workout is too hard, they will complain also, but will understand it is in their best interests to follow the program.

Advanced swimmers have mastered technique and know that they must give one-hundred percent to practice in order to be competitive on meet day. While they should train in all four strokes, they often favor particular events. An advanced swimmer must pay attention to the details of stroke mechanics, training, and competition strategy. Focusing on details will give one swimmer an edge over another, as well as make the sport more interesting. The advanced swimmer needs to target specific goals and work on strength training both in and out of the water.

Advanced swimmers are often role models for the younger, less experienced swimmers. They give the younger, less experienced swimmer a visual image of how a stroke looks when all the parts integrate; those who learn in a predominantly visual way will mimic movement. Advanced swimmers can inspire others to push their limits and broaden themselves.

Teaching eight-and-unders

This is where all great swimmers begin. Those who start in this age group and stick with it will be strong swimmers. Invest in the development of your eight-and-unders, for they are your future team.

It is best to have a separate workout for eight-and-unders, if possible. This way you can work with them in a small group at the desired pace geared towards their age and ability and give them the individual attention needed to develop their strokes. I recommended a short workout—an hour of water time three days per week or preferably forty-five minutes four times a week. After forty-five minutes in the water, swimmers this age usually have retained all they can and stop learning, plus they are physically tired. They can only work so much before they need to have some fun.

Because practice is short, you need to start and stop on time and keep the swimmers continually busy. Schedule this practice when the coach will not have interruptions from pool patrons, parents, older age-group swimmers, other employees, or the telephone. This age group needs constant supervision and should you turn your eyes for a minute they will be all over the place. They are not disciplined enough to do the workout without you.

Focus on technique. Incorporate a lot of teaching into the workout. Run this like an American Red Cross Level V-Level VII class, but with more lap-work. Establish a good crawl. Start with the legs. This may sound elementary, but all young swimmers can improve their kick. Young swimmers should understand key terms such as stretched legs, pointed toes, and a small, quick kick. From where you are standing on deck, you can stretch your arms, point your hands, and

demonstrate a small, quick alternating motion. Tell swimmers to kick a lap and focus on stretching the legs and pointing the toes. Then tell them to kick a lap and focus on a small, quick kick.

"Remember, small quick kick! Go!"

They take off and you watch. If more than one swimmer has a problem performing the skill, repeat the focus one more lap. If one swimmer doesn't get it, but all the rest do, move on to a new skill. You can ask that swimmer to stay after practice for a few minutes to receive individual help. A student may not grasp something right away, but will work on it over time and eventually master it. Allow for trial, error, practice, and accomplishments to happen.

The next day, review by asking them how the legs should be, how the feet should be, whether the kick is small or big, whether the kick is quick or slow. For them to possess the knowledge and feed the information back to you and have this to meditate on while swimming their laps will make them stronger kickers. They need to internalize the knowledge and understand how they should be doing what they are doing rather than just doing it.

Encourage children, be positive, and compliment their success, but also present a challenge, a way for them to become better. What is the one most obvious thing they can do at this moment to improve? Without a challenge, they stagnate, and yet they have so much to learn.

Case study #23

The children are scattered. Michael calls them, but they continue playing. He blows the whistle. They look up and start swimming toward him. He tells them to climb out of the pool and then organizes them in a line on the deck. He wants to pull the group together and accomplish another task. How easily they become inattentive at age seven. He has to keep them moving and busy, but in a structured and guided way.

One student will go first. "Me! Me!" they cry, jumping and waving with unrestrained excitement.

One boy pushes another. The second boy turns and pushes the first boy back.

"Hey!" Michael says and sends them both to the bench to sit for five minutes.

Children will do unsafe things, and accidents can happen. At age seven, they have a lot of energy. They act before they think, and the coach needs to teach them to think first.

Sit this young group down before practice, especially early in the season, when they are newcomers to the team. Position yourself so the students can see you. Make eye contact with everyone, not just those sitting in front of you. Speak loudly, clearly, and at a pace they can follow. Watch the children as you speak; you can usually tell if they are listening. Keep the message simple and brief. Too many lessons in one day will be more than their minds can hold, and they may not hold any of what you say. Yet you can give examples, tell stories, show a picture, and make the lesson enjoyable. Allow them to contribute what they know.

Perhaps the lesson is "Look before you leap." Later that day if a child leaps before looking, address the problem immediately. Then review by repeating the lesson at the beginning of the following practice. Ask the children, "Who remembers what lesson we learned yesterday?"

Michael says, "Let's walk to the shallow end, line up in the water along the wall, and talk about what we are going to do next."

Once they are in the water, he starts them on laps. He can work some of the unfocused energy out of them this way, and then they will more likely rest and listen at the wall.

Teaching swimmers ages nine and ten

This group tends to take learning more seriously than the eight-and-unders. They are open to learning, even eager and enthusiastic, and they are mature enough to grasp concepts intellectually. They absorb much of what you say and try to reason out why things are the way they are or are done in a certain way. They ask a lot of questions.

Ten-and-unders are active; they work and play hard, although play is the more important of the two. Coordination has improved; they can physically accomplish more than they could as an eight-and-under. They want to perform skills well, yet need to be reminded constantly of the task, so that they stay on track and follow through. For example, Nicholas is a typical ten-year-old boy. The initial part of washing a car is exciting, but he loses interest in a short time and plays with the hose.

Begin the season with a low-level workout and a lot of instruction; then increase the yardage per workout as the season progresses, yet always focusing intensively on technique. All swimmers in this age group need stroke refinement; those with more skill will have the edge when racing in a meet. Winning in this age group is less a matter of who is working hardest as it is of who is more technically advanced.

Case study #24

You line your swimmers up at the wall in the shallow end of the pool. Even though they are positioned well, some heads are turned away or are underwater. You say, "One hand on the wall. Heads this way."

Eight out of ten swimmers place one hand on the wall and look your way. You call to the other two students, who either can't hear you, aren't listening, or can hear you, but don't want to do what you are asking of them. While trying to get the two swimmers on track, a third child, who followed your directions originally, lets go of the wall and turns away. You now have the first two on track, but have lost the third. While pulling that child back into focus, you lose a fourth, and so this can go on.

At this point, you must cease all further activity. Once children are in the water for practice, they dislike getting out, especially if they become cold once they are not in motion. But if they will not focus, tell them to sit on the side. Of course, this is always unfortunate for the well-behaved, attentive student. Often, though, this student can help to pull the rest of the group together. This is, after all, a group; when the group is ready, the lesson proceeds.

Once you have everyone's attention at the same time, you must "go for it," because this will not last long. Remember, ten-and-unders are action-oriented and have been in school all day, having done more than their quota of listening; these swimmer are ready to move. Streamline your speech, meaning cut out unnecessary words. Tell the group in a loud, clear, and dominant voice what needs to be done and why, and then get them going.

Teaching swimmers ages eleven and twelve

This is a delightful group to teach. They listen; you don't have to spend so much time on discipline. At this age, they choose to be there or not; no one is making them. The student is willing; motivation comes from within. This makes the coach's job easier, in that you can move beyond the basics into more sophisticated, difficult concepts and skills. You are still a teacher, motivator, disciplinarian, but you are mostly a teacher. Both you and they, because of their maturity, can "get down to business."

Emotionally, though, children in this group are at a vulnerable age and need a lot of encouragement from a coach. They are testing the limits of authority and becoming more independent. The coach needs to treat them like adults and give them more responsibility in their workout. Also, they are influenced by their peers and like to be part of a group. If their friends are swimming, they will stick with it. If their friends aren't, they may lose interest. Yet if a swimmer has been swimming for many years, has had positive experiences, been encouraged, experienced success, then he or she is less likely to drop out, despite what friends are doing. Often a friend or two can be pulled into the sport; thus, you may have the beginning eleven-year-old swim teamer.

Physically, coordination continues to improve as swimmers jump from one age group to the next. Their bodies can handle more intense workouts. The focus on refining strokes never ends, no matter what the age. In addition to that, both coach and swimmer should experiment with race strategies, trying to fine-tune how to swim a particular event. Swimmers usually don't fully understand until they are twelve-and-unders that training hard brings reward. As ten-and-unders they didn't have to work as hard to achieve success. By age twelve, strokes have improved and training appropriately becomes all important in having that edge.

Teaching swimmers ages thirteen and fourteen

This is an awkward age. The emotional vulnerability children felt as twelve-and-unders now grows into an uncertainty about who they are. While they search for their identity by becoming more independent from adults, they lose their identity in becoming more dependent on their peers. Friends become the center of their lives. They are interested in the opposite sex and are exploring these relationships. Children of both sexes are inside of bodies that suddenly don't seem to fit them, and they are self-conscious about it. Being physically fit, though, will help them with their self-image—so the pool is a healthy, wholesome place to be.

If a child has been swimming for many years, this is the point where he or she often makes a decision to stick with it or give it up. You can look at any age-group swim team and see that the numbers begin to drop for boys at age twelve and for girls at age thirteen. At a time in their life when they feel most unsure of who they are and what they want, the sport of swimming becomes more demanding and they need to make a deeper commitment to it. Competition becomes tougher and thus the workouts become harder; more time must be put into the sport in order to do well. Also, a swimmer may feel pressured to be part of the group, and if the group isn't swimming, the swimmer may choose to drop out to be with friends. Boys often want to try other sports—sports that other boys their age are playing—like football, basketball, and baseball.

Teaching swimmers ages fifteen through nineteen

To many fifteen-year-olds, friends mean more than anything else. Sixteen is the age of mobility, when teens become licensed drivers and sometimes own cars. They often look for unstructured, rather than structured places to socialize. The numbers of swimmers in this age group drop, and the commitment levels of those involved drops, as swimmers lead busy lives with school and school activities, friends and perhaps a boyfriend or girlfriend.

The swimmer who stays on the team has to work harder, has to deepen his or her commitment in order to attain success. Does the swimmer want to work as hard as is required to succeed? Or will the swimmer commit to swimming as just one of many things, have fun with it, but not be the best he or she can be? You can assume that those in this age group are experienced, although you might have a beginning sixteen-year-old. Yet he or she will have the maturity to have low expectations in terms of competition.

Train swimmers ages fifteen through nineteen as you would train yourself. The only difference is that they have age on their side and you don't. You cannot recapture this advantageous time of your life in terms of the competitive experience. You can still have good competitive experiences as a master swimmer, but this is their prime. A swimmer in this age group wants more responsibility in the workout, more specialized training, a planned season with specific yardage and higher goals. The emphasis is on conditioning and on shaving times. The coach needs to plan well, vary workouts, and challenge these swimmers, thus holding their interest.

Males and females

Age-group swimmers of both sexes should practice together. This is healthy, for this is the way people integrate in the real world. As far as mental training goes, there is little difference when teaching swimming to a male or female. But gender can determine physical and emotional boundaries. Female athletes, even when they do reduce their body fat, will never be as lean as male athletes. Fat floats, which is a plus in swimming, but weight can also slow an athlete down.

When relating to the emotional side of a swimmer, gender is important in relation to age. For example, the pre-adolescent girl is usually concerned with the relationships with female friends and boys. She will often make decisions based on trying to acquire or maintain popularity. She is experiencing a vulnerable time and needs an empathetic coach. Honest, open communication from adults will give her a sense of acceptance. Coaching her will be quite different from coaching an eight-year-old girl, who is not status conscious, or a seventeen-year-old girl, who has matured beyond needing to fit into a particular crowd.

Division in competition is based on giving each competitor fair odds. Thus, swimmers are divided by age; those who excel in their age group are recognized. They are divided by ability; those of like abilities are placed together, into A, AA, AAA, AAAA categories. They are divided by gender, for so far in the evolution of humanity, male swimmers have been faster than female swimmers in all events. Whether this is entirely due to physical factors, or whether sociological and historical factors play a part, is relative at this point. If women do indeed catch up, divisions based on gender can be reassessed. Until then, swimmers climb up the ladder, from A to AA or from being an eight-and-under to a ten-and-under with gender being the only constant.

Teaching and Learning
Part II

A teaching method: explain, demonstrate, practice

Each individual learns in different ways and at different rates. A coach needs to assess how each athlete learns best and teach to that style. A combination of auditory, visual, and kinesthetic lessons will touch all learners. The American Red Cross trains their Water Safety Instructors to follow a particular sequence—explain, demonstrate, and practice—when teaching a skill. This method works well in a swim team setting, too.

Whether learning occurs during or after verbal instruction depends on both the teacher and student. The teacher needs to deliver the message accurately, clearly, creatively, and must consider the student's age, comprehension level, and in this case physical ability; the student in return must pay attention to the teacher. A teacher should be concerned about whether or not the students are listening and insist on their full attention.

Attention span is affected by various factors. The younger the student, the shorter the attention span. If the message is too complicated or too long, the student loses interest. Give a student one or two things to focus on at a time. Allow one message to sink in before adding more information. Students on overload will become frustrated. You can also clutter what is important with what is unnecessary. The more interesting or relevant the topic, the longer the attention span.

Swimmers learn by watching one another. Typically younger swimmers learn by watching older, more experienced swimmers. This happens naturally, with or without the aid of a coach. Scott is a visual learner. At age five, he goes to the pool daily, playing in the baby pool while his older brother and sister swim on the team. At age six, having never taken swimming lessons, he not only meets the requirements to join the team, but can execute the butterfly and competes all round. At age seven, he wins many blue ribbons and a trophy at the end of the season.

73

When presenting swimmers with a visual image of a skill, it's important to be accurate. Whether the coach or an advanced swimmer on the team demonstrates, ask the group to climb out of the pool to watch from the deck, where they have a better view—and where they are usually more attentive. If a swimmer demonstrates, a coach can talk to the group, reiterating key points. "See the way his head drives forward on the glide."

A video can also be used for demonstation, but younger swimmers will relate better to a live model. Early in the season, I show technique videos (like the *Swim Smarter, Swim Faster* series) to swimmers ages nine through twelve. Mid-season I tape them above and under water from different angles. Older swimmers may be included in this educational process, but eight-and-unders get little out of being videoed. They don't need to see themselves, because they don't know what they are looking at. If you would like your younger swimmers to watch videos, have them watch the Olympians. Let them have a visual experience based on perfection.

When swimmers can't grasp the concept from visual or verbal instructions, you can climb into the pool or ask the students to climb out, and then actually move their limbs to give them a feel for the skill you are teaching. Swim teachers do this a lot in a learn-to-swim program while coaches do it less, especially with older students, who will not want to be taught this way. But sometimes, with your eight-and-unders, there is no other way to get a point across. Sometimes taking a hand and stretching it out or tapping to a point on the palm where the child should feel the push against the water may even be essential to learning.

Practice in itself is the key to good swimming. Swimming many laps in a day will naturally smooth out a swimmer's strokes. A swimmer must find the most efficient way to move through the water. He or she must apply the least amount of effort to travel across the pool in the shortest amount of time. Even a young swimmer will meditate on this while swimming laps, developing a feel for the water per stroke.

The amount of practice needed varies from one individual to the next, which is why repetition is a key ingredient to learning. Repeat drills, and skills that need work, and introduce new concepts to those who have accomplished one step and are ready to move on to the next.

Teaching approaches

American Red Cross Water Safety Instructors teach physical skills through three approaches: whole, part-whole, and progressive-part. When teaching a jump into the water, you take the whole approach, for you cannot divide the skill into parts. If a skill is easy for a particular group of students to execute, then breaking it into parts is unnecessary and time-consuming.

When breaking a stroke into parts (arm stroke, kick, body position, breathing) and working on the parts before combining, you are utilizing a part-whole approach. In the freestyle, the arm stroke can be divided into recovery and power phase. Or you can focus on what the parts of the arm are doing during the recovery and the power phase—moving from fingers to palm, wrist, forearm, elbow, upper arm, and shoulder. The flutter kick can be broken into the up and down beat, the left and right side, or you can move from toe to foot, ankle, lower leg, knee, thigh, and hip. The body position can be divided into right roll and left roll or in and out of the streamline. Breathing can be divided into inhale and exhale in sync with the head roll to the side and down.

Division is a principle of analysis which allows the swimmer and coach to simplify a task, making it more manageable. Swimmers are better able to understand the mechanics of the whole stroke once they understand how the parts work independently and then simultaneously. Focusing on the whole stroke, trying to accomplish everything at once may be mind-boggling for a young swimmer.

When teaching a swimmer to float, then glide, then flutter kick, you are teaching one skill that is built on another and is thus progressive. A swimmer coordinates movement according to his or her ability and thus needs time to evolve. Skill is acquired gradually, through the accomplishment of one step—leading to another and then another.

The coach serves as guide, helping the swimmer to progress by continually revising his or her strokes. The coach must have an exact picture in mind in order to adequately direct the athlete towards the ideal. The more detail-oriented the coach, the better, especially when working with older and experienced swimmers.

Giving and receiving feedback

In order for feedback to be constructive, it must be positive. The coach must care about the athlete and want him or her to progress. All children are in a developmental stage, learning at their own rate. Praise their accomplishments, but do not be false. If a child is executing the breaststroke arms incorrectly, you do not want to say, "Excellent." If he or she places last in a race, you don't want to say, "Great swim." The swimmer will not believe you, and you will lose credibility.

Negative feedback is destructive and hinders learning. Learning should be enjoyable, not intimidating. If a student feels he is being judged or treated too harshly, he will be put on the defensive and may even be unwilling to learn from that teacher. Negativity is discouraging, leads to a loss of confidence, and can be debilitating.

Giving and receiving feedback is a two-way street. First, the student needs to recognize that he or she can learn more and improve. No matter how good a swimmer the student is, he or she can always be better. Secondly, the coach looks at a swimmer and takes in the whole picture, evaluating what is going well and what needs work. Tell the student what he or she is doing well. A student learns just as much, if not more, from accomplishments as from mistakes; accomplishments encourage the child to stick with the sport and progress. Thirdly, don't give a swimmer ten things to work on at once; rather, decide what you think is the most important and work on that. Once you identify the problem, make sure you tell the student how to correct it and give him or her an adequate amount of time to practice. The swimmer masters the skill through practice, then takes the next step in his or her progress.

Case study #25

The coach stands on the deck, watching an eight-and-under swim the crawl. The swimmer's head is raised and stiff, and he needs to relax. He should practice streamlining with the head in the correct position.

The coach does not correct this problem, and the swimmer continues to perform the stroke awkwardly. The longer that bad habits continue, the harder they are to break. Corrections need to be made or the swimmer's progress will be blocked. This is a coach's responsibility. In a small-class situation, a teacher has time to focus on these important techniques, whereas when coaching a large swim team, the problems in one swimmer's stroke can get lost in the numbers of swimmers who are in the water needing attention. Thus, it is important for swimmers to know the basics before entering swim team. The smaller swimmer-to-coach ratio a team can afford—especially for a young team—the better.

Troubleshooting (case study #26)

Ezra executes a windmill stroke above and below the water with his feet dragging, with little or no kick. First, ask him to push off the wall with arms stretched in front and body fully extended. Look for the correct head, body, and arm position. The head position of swimmers will vary because of different buoyancy levels. Ezra may be a Sinker; thus, he will have to lower his head and chest in the water to elevate his legs. Once you have determined that this swimmer is streamline, or in line with the stream of the body's movement through the water, then add the flutter kick. "Explain, demonstrate, and practice" a small, quick kick. Repeat kicking with the kickboard, without a kickboard, on the front, back, and each side, emphasizing streamlining. Developing a power kick will give Ezra confidence, because he will move better through the water. Once kicking power improves, work on the arm pull.

In conclusion

Make sure the concepts that you teach are right, and if you are not sure, teach what you know and research what you don't. You are there to facilitate learning, not to hinder it. Insist that swimmers memorize the parts of each stroke. Work on concepts; then ask your swimmers to give the information back to you. Make them possessors of the knowledge. "I've told you; now you tell me. Explain to me the way the arms work in the crawl. What part of the pull generates the most power?"

Teach not just from a physical, but also a mental reference point. Watching videos, reading handouts, and having discussions adds to what they do in the water. Some swimmers grasp the concepts more quickly than others. They grow, whether you guide them or not. But the better guide you are, the shorter the journey from point A to point B. Young swimmers learn sooner and faster when they have help. Some swimmers go through a whole season, grasping ideas, but not coordinating them. And that is okay. They have more than one season to apply action to concept.

Goal-Setting

Goal-setting defines a swimmer's expectations and directs his or her efforts. If goals are reasonably set—meaning challenging, but attainable—a swimmer should feel more motivated. Proper goal-setting techniques must be learned and take practice to perfect. In taking the time to teach this, you are helping children to focus on that season, as well as setting them up for the future. This will help them with their progress as swimmers and can be applied to other activities throughout their lives. Having a goal means having a target to shoot for, which is different from just doing something for the sake of doing it. Ultimately, you want your swimmers to care about both.

How to set goals

You say, "Goals are important. Let's set some."

Your swimmers say, "Okay," but once in the water they forget all about it. That's why it is important to sit swimmers down to talk about goals and then continue emphasizing this throughout the season. Allow your swimmers to be involved in what directly affects them; they can help you in assessing what is best for them. Also, goal-setting is only beneficial if swimmers believe in their goals and commit to achieving them.

Fifteen minutes prior to an early season practice, ask swimmers to fill out a goal questionnaire. The younger swimmers will need help with this, and the older swimmers on your team can assist. At the next practice, discuss their answers, and set team goals for the season. Compile these responses into a notebook that both you and the swimmers can continually refer to. Add pages so that notes can be taken and adjustments can be made. For the younger swimmers on your team, you can list their goals on notecards and reward their achievements with gold stars.

Writing down goals helps to reinforce them. As the season progresses, goals change, and it is helpful to refer to the beginning of the season not just by trying to remember a discussion, but by being able to look at something set in writing; the direction the swimmer is headed is clarified by reviewing where he or she has been. Reviewing progress can motivate the swimmer; often, he or she may not have fully realized the progress that has been made. Swimmers can also see where their goals are met and not met, and thus, through experience become more accurately able to establish specific and realistic goals for a particular time frame.

Case study #27

Every swimmer benefits from goal-setting, but goals differ from one swimmer to the next. Thus, when setting goals, you have to consider the swimmer's personality and needs. Robby, for example, is a nine-year-old who is active and talented in many sports. He tells his swimming coach that he is thinking of quitting the team because "Laps are boring." The coach talks to him about sticking with the sport for the season and setting goals that will challenge him. They decide to set high goals, because Robby is the kind of child who, when confronted with failure, only becomes more determined and thus pushes harder. He especially enjoys competition, so it is important for him to attend as many meets as possible within a season.

Amy, on the other hand, is a capable ten-year-old who never misses a practice, but refuses to participate in a meet. She enjoys the workout aspect of being on the team, something she can't get anywhere else. The more you push her to go to a meet, the more she resists; if you continue to push, she may drop out altogether. Many teams require participation in meets. Anna needs time and a lot of encouragement. It would also be helpful to talk to her parents. For starters, ask them to go to a meet with her, the goal being to *just watch*.

Set specific goals

Most young swimmers think generally rather than specifically about swimming. They are in the process of learning (from the coach) the specifics—of each stroke, of training properly, and of racing rules and strategies. A good coach knows the details and needs to transfer that knowledge to the students—which takes years. The more detail-oriented a swimmer becomes, the more successful he or she will be.

For example, one swimmer swims twenty-five yards and "just swims." Another swimmer swims twenty-five yards and works on a specific part of the stroke with the sole purpose being to become more proficient. If your goal is to learn, learn the details of each stroke. This in itself will take a lot of time and concentration—and will lead to faster swimming. If faster swimming is your goal, the focus is the same—how to move most efficiently through the water by establishing a base, that base being good stroke technique.

Set realistic goals

What is a challenging, but possible goal for a swimmer when considering his or her age? Are you shooting for a time that is phenomenal for a ten-year-old and out of reach in one season? That will frustrate the swimmer when the goal is, inevitably, not met. It is the coach's responsibility to make sure that goals are reasonable, and if the swimmer still insists on shooting for something unattainable, tell him that you have a lower goal. When the student does not make his goal and does make yours, he cannot be as disappointed. Set realistic goals by evaluating the swimmer's skill level, prior experience, and overall strengths and weaknesses. How motivated is the swimmer? How much time and energy can the swimmer commit?

Whether a goal is set too high or too low, the result is the same: the swimmer becomes frustrated. If the goal is too high, a swimmer may push to the burn-out point to reach it. Either coaches and parents have expected too much of this swimmer or he has expected too much of himself. Even though the swimmer has accomplished the goal, the sport has become too stressful. A goal that you have to work hard to attain can be worthwhile, but this sustained effort takes support from others (parents, coaches). Dedicating oneself to one thing means sacrificing other activities, and even relationships. Life becomes serious at a young age.

If the goal is too low, swimmers may learn, but not to the extent they could if challenged. The swimmer has potential but is not pointed in the right direction and is not pushed hard enough; this is an obvious coaching problem. Most children need external stimulation or will lose interest in an activity. They need direction in order to move forward and cannot ultimately be satisfied when performing at a lower level than they know they are capable of.

Short- and long-term goals

Short-term goals are steps towards long-term goals. When you break a task into parts, it becomes less overwhelming, more manageable, and more possible. When teaching young swimmers, you want to make them more aware of their possibilities. Short-term goals keep a swimmer on track while the long-term goal is the end result.

Long-term goals require continuous work over an indefinite period of time. Anyone who focuses on a long-term goal—and especially a child who is developing, not only physically, but also mentally and emotionally—may lose momentum, enthusiasm, or interest in the goal before ever reaching it. As time passes, many distractions come between the swimmer and the goal, and the distractions may become more worthwhile, for their benefits are immediate. The long-term goal is the pie in the sky. The dreamer is living in the future and shooting high. Sometimes this works; more often, it doesn't.

A long-term goal is in essence "larger than life." A child is used to feeling smaller than the world and as he or she grows the world shrinks; parts of it become more attainable and parts become less so. Often, it is how life is presented to a child that can make a difference between feeling positive or cynical later in life. Do we want to set the child up for disillusionment? No. Yet I believe that dreams are important, for they instill a person with a sense of purpose, which adds meaning to what he or she is doing. Thus, the solution is to focus on the short term, to give the child the chance to feel successful. Allow the dream, but keep it in perspective. Focus on what is possible now; now is a stepping stone to the future.

Goals focused on progress

Goals stimulate a swimmer to think about what is possible when limits are stretched. Progress implies movement (and improvement) from the present to the future. For anyone who is learning—and especially a child—progress of some kind is inevitable. In one season a child can improve strokes, starts, turns; can gain understanding of competitive rules and strategies; can break times. The focus for a young swimmer is on developing skills, and as long as growth is taking place, each swimmer is a winner. If the goal is progress, the swimmer can watch himself succeed. The swimmer works his or her way up a ladder not by focusing on what is at the top, but by focusing on each rung at a time.

Goals that focus on development are within a swimmer's control. Not doing well because he or she didn't train at one-hundred percent can be corrected. To do well without trying hard is an unrealistic expectation. Goals that focus on meet results, people's expectations, or judgements are not within a swimmer's control. To focus on external factors will lead to disappointment.

And yet, if a swimmer fails to place in a meet, I can't guarantee acceptance. Even as a master swimmer I've climbed out of the pool, feeling disappointed with the results. I worked hard and pushed to a goal and expected more. But there is always another chance to do better, too. As for peer comparison, this kind of behavior occurs in both the child's and adult's world. Often, the coach can stop peer comparison, but can't stop a swimmer from feeling what he or she feels. The key is for the swimmer to be aware of his or her disappointment, to look at it for what it is, and then to get rid of it and move on.

I tell my swimmers, "There is also an intrinsic reward in just knowing that you gave a task your full effort, and win or lose, improvement must have occurred. As far as winning or losing, everyone loses at one time or another. But look at the fun you had sharing a day with friends, look at the shape you're in from pushing that hard, look at the fact that you are, despite your perception of loss, a good person and a swimmer with talent."

Teach your swimmers to deal with their disappointments in a positive manner. Use what they assess to be failure to fuel the fire, to keep the passion for the sport alive—and kicking!

Evaluating goals

While setting a goal gives purpose to an activity, the coach needs to give feedback so a swimmer can assess how well he or she is doing in relation to the goal. Young, inexperienced athletes depend on a coach for guidance and recognition. They need someone to design a program they can follow, someone to evaluate their progress and help them reach their goal. As students become older and more experienced, they depend less on the coach and more on themselves, and this is as it should be. But they still need encouragement and guidance so they can continue to learn and improve.

Learning is an endless process. Even master swimmers are happy to have a coach, someone to look at what they are doing from the outside and give them feedback from a different point of view than their own. But a coach cannot force a love for the sport, cannot force a child to commit one-hundred percent to an agreed upon goal. That has to come from within.

Team goals (case study #28)

A letter from Coach Royce, PTSC, 1973: "A coach cannot predict whether a particular boy or girl will be a great swimmer. Years of swimming determine this. Many average swimmers have become outstanding swimmers after years of training; some age-group champions have not excelled later and some have even dropped out of senior swimming. The goals of our club will be the constant improvement of each swimmer. 'C' swimmers will be encouraged to strive for the 'A' level, and 'A' swimmers will be encouraged to strive towards goals which could gain them state or national recognition. PTSC has a program in which you have the opportunity to become a champion. The rest is up to you. No one on the team is a loser. The discipline, training, friendships, and competition are rewards in themselves. In the end, you are really competing against yourself and your own goals."

PART FOUR

Technique

Style versus technique

To swim gracefully, a swimmer must make water his or her element, must spend long periods of time immersed, practicing techniques learned from teachers, adapting them to his or her particular body—in other words, developing a style. Once strokes are mastered per the different sizes and shapes of bodies moving through the water, what distinguishes one swimmer from another is style. Just as we all walk differently, we move differently in the water.

We often teach technique as though there is only one right way, yet as one generation unfolds into another, ideas of what is right or best change. There will always be a swimmer who comes along with a technique that doesn't fit the mold, who will win. Therefore, coaches should teach stroke mechanics with the idea that all swimmers need to internalize what we reason to be the most efficient stroking, kicking, and breathing patterns; but we should also apply the standards of form to each individual's body and mind, and allow for the development of style. I am not talking about breaking a mold, but rather about enhancing each person's technique by considering differences.

As for the swimmer, he or she needs to develop and mature before truly understanding this concept, and thus it becomes the coach's responsibility to guide him or her to that point, not by creating a robot and closing off possibilities, but by making a swimmer adaptable to continual refinement. Thus, as the swimmer ages and becomes more and more responsible for his or her workout, the learning can continue.

The art of swimming is the perfection of movement. Having a winning technique means fine-tuning the details of each stroke, which is definitely possible. This doesn't mean a swimmer is fast, but he or she has all the necessary components to be as fast as possible. The swimmer needs stroke efficiency first, and builds upon that, through training. It takes years to master a feeling for perfection. It takes consistent training to be "the best you can be." A swimmer can only realize this if he or she puts heart and soul into the sport and allows himself the time, energy, and work it takes to get there.

Buoyancy

When a swimmer rests on the water, he or she sinks into it, becoming part of its space. The displaced water has a certain weight, as does the swimmer. If the swimmer weighs less than the water displaced, he or she will float; if the swimmer weighs more, he or she won't. Buoyancy depends on the bone density, muscle, and fat composition of a swimmer. While a light-boned person floats more easily and fat is more buoyant than muscle, you need to look at all three elements in relation to a particular swimmer to truly determine what is affecting his or her buoyancy.

Buoyancy is a factor that all swimmers deal with; thus, a coach needs to educate his or her swimmers about it, so they better understand the relationship between their bodies and the water. Take into consideration that as they grow buoyancy can change. You may want to divide your swimmers into Sinkers, Floaters, and a range in-between. None of these is bad, but considering body types will help you teach swimmers more effectively.

Swimmers can find their buoyancy levels by hanging vertically in the deep end, with their arms glued to their sides and their legs together. They will sink at first, but then their body, acting as a cork in the water, will pop up. They will then continue to bob up and down, until stopping. If they allow this action to take place, when their body comes to a rest, they can find their vertical buoyancy point. Swimmers with deeper buoyancy levels can wear snorkels, so they can breathe under water while waiting for their bodies to come to a rest. Swimmers will find that the more stretched and compact they are, the higher they will ride in the water.

If I choose to demonstrate this drill to my swimmers, they will see the Floater in action. When at rest, the waterline will fall between the bottom of my nose and the top of my lip. I can lay my head back and without moving my arms or legs can breathe for hours. I can find a Sinker to demonstrate the other extreme, and I can find someone who falls in-between; for in a group of students, there will be all types. I tell them that whatever the result, they can all be good swimmers.

Now experiment with buoyancy in the prone and supine positions, adjusting the body to maintain a surface-level float. For the Floater, this will be easy—but be on the lookout for lazy Floaters. They float leisurely on the surface, forgetting to stretch their bodies, squeeze in their muscles, or keep all body parts in line with the spine. The Sinker, on the other hand, needs these key concepts to accomplish the head-to-heel (prone) or head-to-toe (supine) surface position.

Sinkers typically struggle to keep their hips and legs on the surface. One problem may be their form, so that needs to be corrected first. For example, if a swimmer's head is raised above the hairline in the crawl stroke, the feet often sink, and then the swimmer is swimming at an angle. But while Floaters will be able to keep their feet near the surface when they swim with their heads in at the hairline, Sinkers will need to lower their heads further. Because the body needs to stay in line with the spine, when they press their heads down, they will have to press their upper torsos down, too. Sinkers need to imagine a weight pressing the upper torso down, against the water's resistance. The lungs, filled with air and framed by the upper torso, are like any flotation device. When the upper torso and water meet, both pushing against each other, the hips and legs (where muscle is concentrated) pop up. Sinkers also need to relax in the water, for then the body is lighter and floats more easily.

Core control

A swimmer moves beyond buoyancy to core control, which means just what it says: being in control of the core. The core is where the center of mass and the center of gravity meet. This changes and is determined by whether a swimmer is on his or her front, side, or back; whether he or she is streamlined, arched, or tucked; and whether he or she is stationary or moving. In order for a swimmer to be stable in the water, his or her center of mass has to be balanced.

You can observe this principle of balance in a learn-to-swim program. For example, watch youngsters in an American Red Cross Level II class achieve balance on their backs, while floating. Add the kick, and balance changes, as they apply movement to a skill that was stationary. The goal will be to establish core control with a properly executed flutter kick. I have seen children with bicycle kicks on their backs who seem to be in control of their core—until they have to undo the bicycle and move to the flutter. The principle of core control involves maintaining balance when adding limb movements that are correct.

Controlling the core means maintaining balance throughout a stroke (or a start, or a turn). Balanced strokes are more efficient, and efficient strokes are faster. Core control involves maximizing linear movement and minimizing the width of the stroke. A swimmer stretches his or her body lengthwise while becoming as compact as possible. He or she squeezes all the muscles towards the core, thus centering the body from head to toe. In all strokes, the head acts as an anchor, holding the rest of the body in line.

Many swimmers, especially in the past, have put too much energy into moving the limbs of the body and have not focused enough on the power that emulates from the core itself. They need to begin with the core and move the limbs in conjunction with that. This means the body acts as one, with all parts in sync with one another, the core being the center of the action as well as the point of balance.

You can see this concept in all four strokes. In the crawl and the backstroke, the body-roll from side to side empowers both the flutter kick and the power phase of the arm stroke. The more powerful the body-roll, the more powerful the stroke, the more powerful the swimmer. In the breaststroke, you have the wave-like motion of the body; in the butterfly, the body undulates. These strokes reap power from what the core is doing.

The path of least resistance

The most common flaw in all of the competitive strokes is lack of stretch. In my opinion, age-group swimmers can never stretch enough. There's a big difference between being loose and tight and between being stretched and really stretched. By stretching the arm at the catch (in the butterfly, backstroke, and freestyle), a swimmer can apply more force to the underwater pull-push. The breaststroker stretches at the end of the recovery, when streamlining, and then is able to apply more force to the outsweep. Stretching at these points involves not only the arms, but the whole body.

Streamlining means just what it says—to be in-line with the stream. As a stream cuts through land, a swimmer's body cuts a linear path through the water. In order for this body to cut efficiently through water, it must eliminate the resistance that is created when one body meets another—in this case, a solid body meeting a fluid one. The solid body must shrink itself, by compacting its width and stretching its length; thus, we return to the concept of core control.

When a swimmer streamlines, he or she is in either the front or supine position with the arms extended forward, pressing the head just behind the ears. One hand is placed on top of the other, with the thumb of the top hand wrapped around the wrist of the lower hand. This helps to squeeze the arms together. The swimmer stretches his or her arms, as well as the whole body, and looks at the bottom of the pool. A string could run through the core, from the top of the head to the tip of the (pointed) toes, and be pulled at each end, stretching and aligning the body. In addition to that, the swimmer squeezes all of his or her muscles towards the core, creating a compact position.

Swimmers can practice streamlining on the deck. They stand straight, place both arms in the air, then press their head between their arms, placing one hand on top of the other. Make sure their arms press the head in the right sport, and check the hand position. Emphasize the importance of squeezing tightly, as that creates less drag. Now ask your swimmers to practice streamlining in both the prone and supine positions by pushing off the wall, stretching, and traveling as far as possible without arm or leg movement. The more stretched they are, the farther they will glide.

After the push-off, they glide so far before needing some movement. The idea is, yes, they need to move, but in doing so they want to stay as close to the streamline as possible (to minimize drag). Any movement outside of the streamline should be brief, close to and in line with the body, and should create propulsion or lift.

Drag

Drag is the appropriate term for what happens when the body meets the resistance of the water; it drags, or slows down. You can move your arm through the air, and then through the water, and feel the difference. Drag commonly refers to a situation where resistance is maximized, and the result is a loss of force. The goal is to eliminate resistance (as much as possible) and increase force. Of the two, many coaches believe that eliminating resistance is the most important. Thus, we need to look at the three types of drag—friction, form, and wave—and determine how they can be reduced.

Friction drag results when water passes over a rough surface. The rough surface creates friction, which slows down the swimmer. Sources of friction drag are: rough skin, hair, and swim suit fabric. Swimmers reduce friction drag by wearing thin caps and skimpy, thinly textured swim suits with few seams. They shed anything extra—jewelry, for example—that they have on their bodies. They don't need to carry the weight and deal with the added friction. Goggles worn while racing should be small and light. Elite swimmers shave hair off their bodies and legs (but not forearms), but in my opinion this is not necessary for age-group swimmers. I would never encourage it unless the swimmer was at the collegiate or Olympic level and chose to do it.

Friction drag is passive, because it affects speed in a minor way. Yet it is important, for the more you can eliminate any kind of resistance, the better. Cut the corners and they add up. As speed increases (and decreases), drag forces do, too; thus, consistent speed is best.

Form drag relates to the resistance that the form of a swimmer's body creates when it moves through the water. All swimmers, no matter their size or shape, will encounter some drag simply due to the fact that they are a body moving through water. This type of drag is passive, because it is common to all swimmers.

Form drag becomes active when it results from improper technique. Something about the swimmer's form is slowing him or her down. Correct the form, and the swimmer will experience less drag and be faster. Streamlining is the best way to reduce form drag. The thinner and longer the shape, the less resistance. Movement of the limbs must occur at or close to the streamline. Thus, minimize vertical and lateral movements; focus on a horizontal path.

Also, consider core control in reducing drag. Swimmers use the body roll (crawl, back), the wave (breast), and undulating (fly) so that they do not swim flat through the water. In the crawl and backstroke, by rolling continually from side to side a narrower shape moves forward through the water. In the butterfly and breaststroke, while the width of the body remains the same, the swimmer travels over and under the surface rather than confronting the surface head on.

Wave drag results when a swimmer swims in turbulent water. He or she can experience the two extremes when swimming in an ocean and when swimming in a pool. Obviously, swimming in a pool will be easier. Yet when in a pool, water can be more or less turbulent, and the less turbulent it is the easier it is to swim through. Wave drag is active, because it affects a swimmer's speed in a major way.

Wave drag results when improper technique causes turbulence, although there are times when the pool water is moving for other reasons—such as waves created by other swimmers, lack of lane lines, or certain gutter systems. Technique-related movements that cause wave drag:

• **Too much vertical movement.** An example: lifting too high out of the water in the fly. A swimmer only needs to lift high enough for the mouth to clear the water. In all strokes, he or she should think long and avoid bouncing.

• **Too much lateral movement.** Swimmers reduce lateral movement by holding their bodies in line. The head acts as an anchor for the spine. An example: The hips sway in the crawl or backstroke when the swimmer catches the water too close to the midline. This makes it difficult for the body to roll in line and as one unit. The catch needs to occur in line with the shoulders.

• **Movements outside the body's horizontal path (or the streamline).** An example: catching outside shoulder width in the crawl or backstroke. The swimmer won't be able to execute a long, clean hand entry. This will result in a short, choppy stroke, which will generate waves.

• **Splashing the water.** Swimmers must think smooth, relaxed, and gentle throughout the recovery and especially at the catch, and try to create as few waves as possible.

Breathing

All beginning swim teamers need to feel comfortable submerging, blowing out their mouths and noses, and opening their eyes. These are pre-swim-team skills. They also need to know that swallowing water or getting it up their noses happens occasionally and is a minor discomfort that passes. Even experienced swimmers can hit a wave with their mouths open and accidentally swallow water.

When floating on the back, swimmers can maintain a normal breathing rate. Most swimmers, when floating on their front, will opt to hold their breath for longer and come up for air when necessary, and before gasping. The American Red Cross once taught a skill called survival floating, which was based on this concept. The survival float emphasized relaxing in the water and maintaining a comfortable breathing rhythm (in and out). In an aquatic emergency, a person could continue this for a long time—and survive.

When swimming, the need for oxygen increases. The survival float pace may equal that of an easy swim, but as the heart rate goes up, so does the need for oxygen. This can be compared to the breath needed when walking as opposed to the breath needed when running. When racing, a swimmer will inevitably deal with oxygen depletion. Setting a pace minimizes this hazard. The swimmer sets up a breathing pattern so that from the beginning to the end of a swim he or she has enough air. Otherwise, once the swimmer loses oxygen, he or she also loses energy—and quickly.

Breathing should be part of the movement of a stroke, and should not slow a swimmer or require any extra energy. The swimmer does not have to move a body part out of its normal path to find air. In the backstroke, the swimmer breathes in and out, as he or she regularly would when moving through air. One possible rhythm: breathe in when one arm recovers; breathe out when the other arm recovers. With the other three competitive strokes, the swimmer breathes when the body moves into a specific position. In the crawl, he or she breathes when the body rolls to the side. In the breaststroke, he or she breathes every cycle, when in the prayer position, before the lunge. In the butterfly, he or she breathes when the body lifts after the finish of the power phase. To breathe at any other than these particular spots will require added movement, which will require energy, and a swimmer will tire faster.

A common problem with young swimmers (and perhaps your eight-and-unders) is traveling too far without taking a breath, and then finally breathing and taking in too much air. Tired, they hold their bodies in a stroke's breathing spot for too long. They need to breathe more often, so they don't get into this desperate situation. It's better to breathe less air more often than to breathe too much air less times.

When breathing, swimmers need to exhale the carbon dioxide completely before taking in new oxygen. If they don't exhale completely, they won't get a full breath of air, will take in less oxygen, and thus will tire sooner. For example, if they have set up a three-stroke-and-breathe pace in the crawl stroke, they may not even make it to the third stroke. Yes, they can breathe after two, but then they have lost their breathing rhythm. Humans need oxygen to sustain their life, and when on land we breathe in and out continually, often without thinking much about it. It needs to happen this way in the water, too. Swimmers need to set a breathing and stroking rhythm that fits the distance they must travel and the amount of oxygen they need.

Hand power

In all strokes, hands play a crucial part throughout the recovery and power phase. They are either pulling, pushing, or slicing, and at all times are contributing significantly to the motion forward. As a boat needs a paddle and needs the paddle pitched at a certain angle to insure movement in a certain direction, the swimmer needs the hands. I emphasize sculling drills, to give swimmers a feel for the power that can emulate from the hand alone. The power phase of each stroke is essentially a scull; thus, sculling drills will help swimmers improve what they are doing under the water.

A swimmer needs to master buoyancy concepts before executing sculling drills. The body is not going to move effectively through the water with the hands alone propelling it unless the swimmer has established a surface position. Thus, first things first. Sculling also helps the swimmer to get a feel for keeping the body in line and stretched. The core of the body needs to be centered. If loose and out of line, a swimmer won't be able to propel his or her body very quickly forward. With core in control, and in a surface position (either prone or supine), the swimmer pitches the palms (which are stretched and flat) at a particular angle and pushes the water so the body moves either forward or backward.

Once swimmers master the following sculls, executing them fast (but without creating waves) will develop tremendous hand power. Prone sculls: lobster, canoe, alligator. Supine sculls: standard (head first or foot first), dolphin, or torpedo. The torpedo scull works especially well when a swimmer wants to scull fast. Sculling also makes for an excellent cool down.

Getting the feel

"Getting the feel" (for the freestyle, backstroke, breaststroke, or butterfly) is a great slogan for young swimmers. Introduce this concept to age-group swimmers by talking about it frequently; plaster it on the swim-team bulletin board.

They react. "What does it mean, coach, to *feel* each stroke?"

Not only do swimmers need to learn how to execute a stroke correctly, but they also need to *feel* power from their movements. For example, if a swimmer pitches the hand at the right angle, catches the water, and attains power, this gives him or her a sense of unequaled satisfaction. Feeling the right spot empowers a swimmer mentally as well as physically. Not only does the swimmer look good, but he or she also feels good.

A stroke can look technically correct, but not be powerful. Power results from looking beyond the surface of a particular concept, such as the six-beat kick, and actually experimenting with it enough to know that it works--and better than anything else. Once a swimmer has learned a skill, his or her attention should shift to increasing its power. A swimmer has to mentally climb inside a skill to find its power. And a coach needs to remind a swimmer that feeling is important. When a swimmer clicks with a movement, ask him, "Did that feel different?" Or, "Can you feel more power from doing it that way?"

Whatever the stroke, whatever is moving—body, arms, legs—when a swimmer feels the power once, he or she knows what to shoot for again, knows when he or she has hit it, and knows when he or she hasn't. In the process, the swimmer has developed an intelligent feel for what is working, what is not, and why or why not.

A coach can help a swimmer to accomplish a particular skill by verbalizing and demonstrating it correctly, and by allowing for practice and providing feedback. A coach can be a swimmer's eyes, but cannot feel what a swimmer is feeling. This sense has to come from the swimmer.

Thinking technique

A good coach must give swimmers the proper information to intellectualize the stroke. If swimmers can intellectualize how and why, they have more of a chance of success. The more they know, and the more comfortable they are with the knowledge they possess, the better swimmers they will be. Thus, they not only feel a stroke, but also think it. Thinking and feeling are related.

Think about technique during practice, not at a meet. In competition, thinking may hinder a swimmer's performance, because thinking requires energy. While thinking technique in practice is important, too much of a good thing without a break can be stressful. Just as a swimmer needs a physical rest, he or she needs a mental rest, a time to empty the mind, become one with the water and swim for the sake of swimming. Eventually all the hard work, all the concentration on technique leads to natural movement that is both accurate and beyond thought.

Drills are exercises to get a swimmer thinking about technique. They can be done while stationary or while moving, and they involve isolating parts of strokes so that swimmers can learn key concepts. They provide repetition, which is essential to learning, and they provide variety, so that if one way of learning doesn't work, maybe another way will. Drills help swimmers acquire a feel for a movement and also develop strength.

Butterfly

Body position

The dolphin action is a series of arcs through the water. The body arcs over the water when recovering; the body arcs the opposite way (in an arch) as the hands push towards the waist and out at the thigh. This wave-like or undulating motion propels the body forward and creates fewer waves than a flat stroke; and the more fluid the arcing motion, the less wave drag. Swimming flat is similar to swimming in rough surf while undulating is similar to what the dolphin does; in imitating the dolphin, you become the wave.

A drill for the body: Swimmers tie their legs together and do not use them; they use only their arms and let their bodies undulate. Executing the arm stroke without the kick shows a swimmer how much momentum he or she can achieve when undulating the body.

The arm stroke

The Recovery: Both arms lift out of the water when the hands break the surface at the thighs, pinkie fingers leading and thumbs exiting last, meaning the palms face towards the torso and each other. As the arms arc to the catch position, the shoulders and upper back also arc, but forward and down. The arms should be straight, or nearly straight, and relaxed. The thumbs point towards the surface throughout the recovery, meaning the palms become visible to a coach watching a swimmer from the rear and the side. The swimmer should not be able to see his or her hands as they catch, because the chin is squeezed to the chest. The hands are pitched at a 45° angle, thumbs entering first.

The catch occurs in line with the shoulders. Catching closer in destroys the rhythm. Catching farther out adds width and drag to the stroke; streamlining principles involve minimizing width while maximizing length. Thus, a swimmer must full extend at catch. In putting the whole body into this moment, he or she is propelled forward briefly in a power glide. The swimmer, when stretched at the catch, will be able to apply more force to the power phase. The effect is similar to stretching a rubber band and then letting go.

The Power Phase: From the catch, the arms travel to a depth of at least ten inches. The pull begins with the shoulders under the water. The palms press out, but not too wide, before pivoting in and pressing towards the waist. When pressing in, the upper arms stay close to the surface while the lower arms travel under the elbows, which bend. The flat and hyper-extended palms, acting as paddles, push through under the body, so the elbows don't exit early. Once the palms pass the waist, they pivot out, and the elbows straighten as the thumbs almost brush the legs. The hands accelerate through the finish and into the recovery.

In summary: When recovering, the thumbs are down as the hands exit the water after the finish. The arms arc over the water at the same time, one half of the body mirroring the other half. At the catch, the thumbs enter first and the swimmer stretches the arms, as well as the whole body. Underwater, the flat of the hands push in an hourglass shape. I think of the underwater phase (from the catch to the finish) as similar to throwing a baseball. A swimmer grabs the water at the catch and throws the ball, following through to the finish with the same kind of force.

Teaching the arm stroke

Most beginners weigh their ability to do the fly on how their recovery looks or feels, when in actuality the focus of an arm stroke should fall on the whole cycle rather than one part, especially when the *power* phase refers to what happens under the water. While I like to break a stroke up into parts and work on the details, I don't want students to lose sight of the concept of a stroke being a cycle, a whole fluid motion.

I will not even teach arms to my young swimmers until they have coordinated the dolphin kick adequately and are strong on the front, sides, and back; until their bodies are in line when streamlining; and until they are in control of both aspects of the arch motion that comes with the first and second kick. Through the instructions and drills, I also require an understanding of what they have accomplished.

When teaching the arm pull, I introduce the pull buoy. This will keep their legs together. And they don't need to think about the kick; we can concentrate on the arms. The legs will naturally kick, to keep the body afloat, but they will kick in unison, because of the pull buoy. Thus, while students are working on arms, their legs will be doing whatever, but that whatever will be natural and similar to the actual kick. The pull buoy will sink slightly when the body arches and the knees bend.

There are various ways to go about teaching the arms, none of which will be easy at first for

a beginner. But you can make it fun. Strength is needed to lift both arms out of the water at the same time. Many young swimmers will be using muscles they haven't used before and will need time to work these muscles before being able to execute the skill well. Thus, many coaches believe in one-arm fly drills for young swimmers. They can develop the concepts of the stroke one arm at a time, can work on undulating the body and synchronizing the kick with the arm stroke. If you like the one-arm drill, practice the same amount of yardage on one side as the other, so that both sides of the body are worked out equally.

I occasionally incorporate one-arm fly drills into a workout as a learning experience and for variety, but do not advocate a lot of it, for I feel I am training the minds of my young swimmers to ultimately feel the wrong thing. The one-arm fly drill takes the focus off of the forward momentum, the wave arching in and out, and makes swimmers "think" side, which is how they think when swimming the freestyle and backstroke. One of the things I find so refreshing about the fly is breaking out of that side-to-side pattern. I like the feeling that both arms and both feet are one, not two. If anything, one side mirrors the other, but a big part of it is that they work together as a unit and cannot be separated. You just can't take a butterfly and clip one wing without damaging its mentality as well as its physical reality.

I teach two arms from the beginning, although I realize that the two arms arching over the water will be physically hard for young swimmers. We work on short distances. We work on one key thing at a time—what I call "having a focus." The focus this time is to catch the water in line with the shoulder—not too far out, not too far in—thumbs first. This is a kind of meditation; all other thoughts are blocked out. We think one thing and one thing only.

We work on underwater only—a sculling drill with the face in the water and arms stretched forward and in line with the shoulders. Swimmers push the hourglass pattern to the thighs. We practice this vertically, on the deck and in the shallow end; we practice this by pushing off the

wall, streamlining, and performing one scull; we practice this by moving across the pool, stopping after each scull by placing the feet on the pool bottom, then pushing off, stretching to the catch position, and sculling again.

The dolphin kick

Throughout the arm stroke, both legs remain glued together, acting as one leg. The up and down movement originates from the hip and thighs, and the toes point throughout. On the downbeat the tops of the feet push against the water while on the upbeat the bottom of the feet push against the water. The knees bend slightly on downbeat and straighten on the upbeat.

A butterflyer dolphin kicks twice per arm cycle, once at the catch and once at the finish. The difference in the two kicks lies in their size, the degree of leg extension, the position the rest of the body is in when they are executed, and the depth in which they occur. The catch kick occurs when the swimmer is streamlined while the finish kick occurs at the finish of the pull, when the upper torso arches; thus, the catch kick occurs closer to the surface than the finish kick. The legs fully extend when kicking at the catch in contrast to kicking at the finish, when they bend more. The slightly smaller second kick helps lift the arms out of the water, helps to begin the recovery.

Kicking drills

A strong kick is essential to being a strong butterflyer. The kick is something that young age group swimmers can learn, can develop, and should work on often, as part of every workout.

• Vertical kicks: Swimmers are in the deep end, in a vertical position, dolphin kicking for X minutes—either with the arms glued to the side, crossed at the chest, or held out of the water. Always give the swimmers something specific to do with their arms. All parts of the body have a roll to play, no matter what the skill is that you are teaching. Make sure that the body remains vertical and in line.

• Kick ups: Swimmers execute a foot-first surface dive in the deep end, touch the bottom, and dolphin kick (fast) to the surface.

• Underwater kicks: Work in an area that is three to five feet deep and ask your swimmers to kick along the bottom of the pool. Many of the younger swimmers will float up and actually be kicking on the surface eventually, and the drill calls for them to be underwater. By asking them to kick along the bottom, you give them specific information on where you want them to be and also challenge them. Try this drill with the arms glued to the side and with the arms streamlined.

• On the back: Swimmers push off the pool wall, streamlining and dolphin kicking to a specified distance—say the backstroke flags—and then angle to the surface. You can move the flags farther from the side as swimmers improve.

• On the side: Dolphin kicking while balancing on the side helps a swimmer work on keeping the body in line. Swimmers become more aware of the hips and thighs contributing to this kicking action. Emphasize kicking both ways.

• With equipment: Dolphin kicks with a kickboard seem to only accent the streamline kick, not the position of the legs or body on the second kick. When practicing with the board, the catch kick is not completely streamlined, because the head is raised, which does not occur in the actual stroke. The finish kick can only be accurately executed if a swimmer places the board behind the back and holds it with both hands. Then he or she practices finish kicks only, whereas the actual motion consists of the catch kick and finish kick, one then the other.

I avoid using a kickboard with the dolphin kick and advocate both aquafins and monofins—or just the body itself, without any equipment. Both aquafins and monofins make the leg muscles work harder. Aquafins are good for holding a young swimmer's feet together while still maintaining the feeling the two feet actually have while kicking. The monofin exaggerates the kick, giving the swimmer a different feel. Exaggerating or changing the feel of a movement can create an awareness of the actual movement. Kicking with the large, heavy monofin emphasizes the hip action, so that when the fin is off, the hips—and thighs—exert the same amount of force, but with only two small legs to push together through the water. The legs now feel light and move with such ease. This is a thrill the first time you experience it! Monofins also press on the toes and develop a stronger arch. After working out with a monofin, the toes feel glued in an extreme pointed position.

• One kickboard drill: Swimmers stretch their arms forward and hold the kickboard perpendicular to the surface. Dolphin kicking against this added resistance provides a swimmer with an isometric activity that will make the kick more powerful.

Breathing

A swimmer needs rhythm to accelerate. A lot of this comes from developing a breathing cycle that works in sync with the arms and legs. For some butterflyers that may mean breathing every stroke; for others it may mean breathing every two or three strokes. Distance flyers breathe more frequently than sprint flyers.

Head position is vital in all four strokes, for what the head does will determine whether the body is in line with the movement—which is essential. The head position in the fly can easily determine one swimmer's speed over another's. The head lift occurs as the hands push and

stretch at the finish of the power phase. That push and stretch actually lift the head up. But the head should lift only high enough so that the mouth clears the water. The swimmer grabs a quick, but good breath. During the recovery that follows, the head drives forward and down in line with the body, which is also driving forward and down, past the catch. The head drive can be considered part of streamlining—for in streamlining, the whole body takes part in the stretch.

Many young flyers lift their heads too high for too long, pausing at the finish of the power phase. Because the stroke requires strength, young swimmers tire out and mistakenly think they need more air. They want to rest, but it's actually more tiring to pause at this point; it's tiring to hold the head up and the body in an arch for long. A pause in this arched position will only slow momentum and make it harder to lift the arms up out of the water and keep going due to static versus dynamic inertia. It's easier to move from an already moving state than from a static state. Swimmers must catch a breath, continue, and relax on the recovery and when stretching at the catch. Also, applying force to the finish is a critical part of the power phase. Not only does this push at the finish lift the head up, it also enables the arms to continue into the recovery. For a swimmer to pause in a spot where he or she should be applying the most force means not getting the maximum benefit out of the fly movement.

A coach can give swimmers short-distance drills focused solely on breath control, head drive with recovery, stretch, stretch. In the count, you can hear the rest. Give swimmers a count for everything. This teaches them to focus on timing—and to understand timing—much like we learn a dance through focusing on beats, with or without a song. Any movement has a count. Here you are synchronizing the body parts to one another, which is essential for a stroke to be smooth and fluid.

Training with the snorkel: Normally, the breath is built into the undulating motion of the stroke. To have to keep the head down challenges the swimmer to work on undulating without the head, a key figure in the equation. Working with the snorkel teaches the body to contribute more to the movement. Later, when you factor the head back in, the stroke is stronger and more fluid. This training is helpful for sprinters, who may not want to breathe every stroke, but also helpful for distance swimmers in that it develops cardiovascular endurance.

Side versus forward breathing

Side breathing with the fly is possible, but considered unorthodox. Supporters of side-fly breathing say that it minimizes vertical movement. I believe that to roll the head to the side may minimize vertical movement slightly, but to an insignificant degree. Some vertical movement in the fly is necessary if we want the body to undulate, which we have already determined is more efficient than not undulating because it reduces wave drag. The answer is to eliminate vertical movement as much as possible; in other words, the head lifts high enough to catch that quick breath and no more. Choose a little vertical movement over a lot of oppositional movement.

By oppositional movement, I refer to the head as the anchor point in every stroke. Side breathing contradicts the idea that the body should always stay in line. Form drag results when a swimmer moves out of alignment. A swimmer is either going to raise the head minimally to breathe, or he or she is going to throw the head to the side, in opposition to what the body is doing.

Rotating the head to the side, in opposition to the body's waving movement forward, is not only awkward, but also takes more energy than moving the head in unison with the rest of the body. The finish of the power phase lifts the upper torso, whether a swimmer breathes there or not, and the more force applied to the finish, the easier the lift will be. To resist the natural movement will take more energy than to go with the flow. When throwing the head to the side, a swimmer risks using more energy, all to save minimal, if any, vertical movement.

Swimmers who choose to side-breathe should breathe bilaterally rather than to one side. The reason: to keep the stroke balanced and not to overuse one side. At the same time, if they alternate sides with each breath, their timing will be thrown off. Thus, they can breathe three times on one side and three times on another, or one lap on one side and one lap on the other.

Timing

I use a count of four for the butterfly. A count of eight is too slow for practice and definitely for the race. A count of eight is even unrealistic for the synchronized swimmer, because butterfly is a hard stroke to slow down. Count one and two for the recovery, with the stress (the catch kick) falling on two; count three and four for the power phase, with the stress (the finish kick) falling on four.

Training the butterflyer

If the fly is a swimmer's goal, he or she needs to do a lot of it. To develop the strength needed to race in this stroke, a swimmer needs to over-distance train. Thus, while strength is needed to execute the stroke efficiently, fly racing requires additional work. When competing, a swimmer wants to have the strength to go the distance plus more.

For age-group swimmers in particular, this is one stroke that when it breaks down, it really breaks down. Most coaches believe that it is not beneficial to have a swimmer continue to swim a broken-down stroke. Once the swimmer reaches that point, stop, rest, and then go again. Thus, in many practices you see either fly drills, for learning purposes, or fly sprints, which match the younger age-group swimmer's endurance level. Of course, there is a big difference in terms of which end of the age-group spectrum the swimmer happens to be on and what his or her level of experience with the stroke is. For advanced age-group swimmers, for those who have mastered the fly technique, I advocate some distance fly work.

So you want to be a butterflyer...

Only a small portion of age-group swimmers will have this goal. It is not that this stroke is harder than the others, as many of them will tell you. It is just that a large part of being able to coordinate the butterfly takes having a certain level of experience in the water and having the strength to do it. Thus, when teaching the stroke to young swimmers, it's important to focus on both coordination and strength drills. This will take time, and thus many of them will tell you the stroke is hard.

In order to execute this stroke well, a swimmer needs to be strong. Various drills will help the beginner to move in the direction of mastery, but even if a swimmer masters the coordination of the stroke, he or she will not become fast without practicing a lot. Thus, the swimmer who competes in the butterfly must incorporate the stroke into each workout. There are so many freestylers, because so many of our workouts are freestyle-based. Freestyle is less stressful on the body than the other strokes and establishes a good base. A swimmer needs a strong freestyle before he or she can move into a strong fly. While a beginner can and should practice fly drills geared to his or her skill level, the stroke only truly works for those who spend time with it; it's for the advanced. But the advanced swimmer had to start somewhere in order to progress.

Some bodies will adapt better to this stroke than others. While in the crawl and backstroke, we talk about the tall and lean swimmer with long arms, here is a stroke for a shorter, stockier person, someone with muscular thighs, but flexible legs and backs. If you can generalize, butterflyers tend to have large shoulders and broad backs.

In summary: If a child has an interest in the fly, it is always good to start young. But the potential will not fully be reached until he or she has developed a certain level of experience with the stroke. The butterfly does not just snap into place, but needs time and patience, perhaps more than any other stroke.

An age-group coach must give his or her swimmers the base to become good at this stroke in the future. Make sure you are teaching the stroke accurately; focus on detail, especially as swimmers improve. Since so much of the stroke is timing, drills focused on developing strength are just as important as drills focused on coordination. You can teach your young swimmers to perform this stroke well. But it is the swimmer who connects with the stroke, who is pushed over a fine line into loving the stroke, who will want to do it often, who will have the patience to develop with it, who will truly become the master.

Backstroke

Body position

When swimming the backstroke, the body is always in motion, rotating from side to side. All parts rotate as a unit on an imaginary line running from the center of the top of the head, through the core of the body, and out between the two feet. The swimmer needs to be as stretched lengthwise as possible; thus, imagine a string pulling him or her from head to toe. The swimmer also needs to be as compact as possible; thus, squeeze all the muscles (and especially the buttocks) towards the midline.

When rolling, drive the hips from right to left and left to right. Roll to one side until the underside of the opposite shoulder breaks the surface. Meanwhile, the head remains stationary, locked tightly in line throughout the stroke. The head is the anchor, holding the rest of the body in place.

Teaching body position

To teach body position, you need to teach body alignment, core control, and how to rotate on an imaginary axis. Begin by asking swimmers to stand straight (on the deck), looking ahead at a spot (on the wall). They press their arms to their sides and keep their feet together. They press their shoulders back, but also down, and stretch their elbows. The buttocks need to be squeezed in.

Ask them to imagine a string running through the core of their bodies and to imagine the string pulled at both ends, so the body is stretched from head to toe. If they bend at the waist, or lift the head to look around, the body is no longer in line. If the head is too high or the legs are too deep, the body moves forward at an angle; thus, more of the body makes contact with more of the water, which means more drag. Remember, when streamlined you move forward with the least resistance and the most efficiency.

Now ask swimmers to hold this aligned body position, but slowly turn to the right, taking baby steps. As they turn 360°, ask them to feel an imaginary weight pressing on both the chest and right shoulder. As the weight presses down, the right shoulder turns and the left shoulder follows.

Your swimmers will be glad to know that "it is time to try this in the water." I like to use the deep end for this next lesson, although that is not necessary. Ask your swimmers to float on their backs, aligning their bodies on the surface. Sinkers will have trouble with this, and you can attach a small float to their ankles. Ultimately, Sinkers need to work on balancing their bodies in the water, which is a lesson that should precede this one.

Ask swimmers to stretch their bodies, to feel someone pulling each end of the string. Some pools have underwater speakers with microphones, which helps, for swimmers have their ears in the water and you can direct them to the next step without them having to stop and then realign themselves. You can teach the lesson without speakers, but it will take more time. Between each step, you will have to call the swimmers to the edge while you explain what comes next.

For now, though, you are still working on alignment and core control. The arms press the sides, the legs stay together, the buttocks are squeezed, the waist is flat, and the shoulders press back and down. With this accomplished, swimmers execute the turn in the water. They feel an imaginary weight, pushing the right shoulder down and lifting the left shoulder up. The whole body, including the head, stays in line throughout the turn—past 90 to 180°. Here, face down, swimmers sometimes get stuck. To resolve this, they must continue to feel the weight pressing the right side of the body, but also must feel someone on each end of the imaginary string pulling both ways. Stretching here is instrumental in lifting the whole body past 270 to 360°.

This drill is a synchronized swimming figure called the log roll. No kicking is allowed. The body must do all the work. The skill teaches key backstroke concepts and should be repeated until swimmers master it perfectly.

Other drills for the body roll

• Swimmers swim a lap of backstroke, balancing a pair of goggles on the forehead. While the body rolls in-line from side to side, the head remains stationary.

• Run a rope parallel to the wall of the pool, only allowing the swimmer enough room to swim on the side. The swimmer must swim between the wall and the rope without touching either and can only do this by rolling from side to side, not by swimming flat. The body will have to be streamlined, and the arms will have to move close to the body. In this way you create a tight backstroke.

The flutter kick

When flutter kicking, the legs alternate as they move back and forth. The swimmer kicks from the thighs, with legs stretched, knees relaxed, and toes pointed. The top of the foot pushes up, and the bottom of the foot pushes down. The ankle remains loose, so the foot can push back and forth. The swimmer executes a small, quick kick; a large kick will create drag as the legs move farther from the streamline.

The kick is important in relation to the body position, which rotates; the kick should propel the body forward and also from side to side. Aim for three kicks per side (or per stroke), or six kicks per stroke cycle. The kick propels the body like a motor propels a boat. If the motor is under the stern and the bow is pointed up, the boat will not be balanced. Moving forward, it could flip over. Thus, the body must be balanced in order for the kick to be effective.

Back kicking drills

• Flutter kick while streamlining: The arms extend, with the elbows straight and the hands together. Swimmers squeeze the upper arms to the head, just behind the ears.

• Flutter kick while squeezing the arms to the sides: While rolling from side to side, swimmers keep their heads stable and their bodies in line. The whole shoulder should surface when the body rolls.

• Flutter kick while balanced on one side: The lowest arm extends and the head lay flat against it; the upper arm squeezes the side.

• Stroke with one arm only: Swimmers still kick and roll on both sides. For example, during the first half of a right arm recovery, the swimmer is lying on his or her left side. When the stretched arm reaches a point in midair that is perpendicular to the body, the third kick on the left side along with hip drive pushes the body toward the right, so that it can follow the right arm to the catch and below. Normally, the left arm begins its recovery, but in this drill it doesn't; thus, the swimmer can focus on what the right arm is doing under the water. During the last half of the power phase, the right hand passes the waist, flips, and pushes down below the hips before lifting again. During this part of the power phase, the body begins its roll back to the left side, a roll that will continue as the right arm lifts again until reaching midair (90°).

• Swimmers flutter kick ten times on the right side (streamlining with the lower arm extended and the upper arm squeezed to the side), then backstroke with the left arm. They flutter kick ten times on the left side, then backstroke with the right arm. Emphasize small, quick kicks. On the next lap, they flutter kick eight times on one side, stroke, eight times on the other side, stroke. Next, six kicks, stroke, six kicks, stroke; then four kicks, stroke, four kicks, stroke; and finally, three kicks, stroke, three kicks, stroke.

• A six-beat kick without arms: With practice, young swimmers should be able to accomplish a six-beat kick on each side. They have to hold the body on each side, longer than is natural, but this will help them with balance while developing a side kick and body roll. They can work on stretching and keeping the body in line.

• A four-beat kick without arms: A four-beat kick on each side without the arms is manageable for your intermediate age-group swimmers.

• A three-beat kick without arms: The arms help speed the body up to point where three-beat kick is realistic rhythm. Without the arms to propel a swimmer forward at the usual rate, some other part of the body has to compensate in order to move forward efficiently. With the arms glued to the torso and without the aid of any equipment, swimmers drive the hips from side to side and kick hard—especially with that third kick—in order to roll without losing forward momentum. They won't make it to the other side unless they thrust the hips in the direction of the roll.

Older, more advanced swimmers will be able to coordinate this move, although they will most likely lose forward momentum at first and for awhile—until they practice it often. Young swimmers will have difficulty executing three beats on each side without arms, without fins, and without losing forward momentum.

• A three-beat kick without arms, but with flippers: With flippers or zoomers on, swimmers can compensate for the propulsion missed without the arm movement and easily execute the three-beat kick per side and move forward efficiently. You've simplified the stroke in cutting the arms, yet swimmers still experience propulsion; thus, they can focus on body stretch and alignment, core control, and rolling in line, as a unit. When wearing fins, the swimmer pushes a bigger foot through the water; this takes more muscle, and thus practicing with fins develops the leg muscles. Fins create a more flexible foot and ankle and a strong toe point, all of which enhances the flutter kick.

Swimmers tightly glue their arms to their sides (no loose elbows), so they are out of the way. In this way, they can isolate and thus focus on the leg movement alone. They focus on the hip drive and on rolling the body in line and as a unit from side to side; on stretching the legs, as well as the whole body; on squeezing the buttocks muscles so the hips roll easier; and on kicking from the hips.

• A three-beat kick without arms, but with aquafins: Once a swimmer masters the three-beat kick, no-arm-stroke drill and wants more of a challenge, he or she can put on the aquafins. Practicing with aquafins adds resistance and thus difficulty. Aquafins do not add propulsion. Without the arms, the swimmer relies solely on the legs to propel him or her forward and from side to side. The swimmer must push harder with that third kick and thrust harder with the hips.

The arm stroke

Let's consider the recurring rule: When moving outside the streamline, lift and propulsive factors need to be engaged. The back arm stroke is propulsive during the power phase and employs lift during recovery. While divided here into recovery and power phase, the back arm stroke is a continuous motion, executed precisely in an unbroken rhythm.

The recovery (the lift component): The thumb leads as the arm lifts from the thigh. The hand is flat and stretched, the palm facing in. Thumb to pinkie are in line with the body as the hand slices through the air. The arm stretches throughout the recovery and especially when reaching that point perpendicular to the body (90°). The eyes spot the thumb, yet the head remains still. The body is on its side at this point. For example, when lifting the right arm from the thigh to the 90° point, the body is on its left side.

At the 90° point, the hand rotates 180°; then the arm continues its arc, traveling close to the ear before catching the water at either the one or eleven o'clock, which is in line with the shoulder and close to the streamline. Also, at the 90° point, the body rolls towards the lifted arm, following its arc to the catch; thus, as the hand turns, the body turns. If the right arm is raised, the body will roll to the right.

Thus, at the beginning of the recovery, the body is on its left side as the right arm lifts from

the thigh to the 90° point. During the second half of the recovery, as the right hand rotates 180°, the body rolls to the right side and continues to roll right as the pinkie proceeds to the catch, at the eleven o'clock.

Recovering on the other side: When the swimmer is partially on the right side, the right shoulder is submerged and the underside of the left shoulder is visible. The rest of the body, having rolled as a unit, is in line with the shoulders. The swimmer lifts the left arm, from where it is stretched beside the thigh, straight into the air. Every part of the arm (from shoulder to elbow to fingertip) should be stretched. While the fingers remain relaxed, the hand itself acts as a paddle.

The catch ends the recovery and begins the power phase. Think of the swimmer as lying on the face of a clock, facing you, the center of his or her head lined up at the twelve and the two feet placed side by side at the six. The right pinkie finger catches at the eleven o'clock, and the left pinkie catches at the one o'clock. Catching farther out than the one and eleven o'clock creates drag and also sets the swimmer up for a less powerful power phase. Catching closer to the midline will make the body weave and become unbalanced; the body will not roll as a unit. If the right hand catches, the swimmer rolls to the right, until the underside of the left shoulder is visible. He or she rolls to the left until the underside of the right shoulder is visible.

The power phase: As the hand descends below the catch, the body continues to roll downward. After slicing the water approximately six inches deep, the hand pivots, so that the palm can push in toward the waist. The elbow bends, adding force to the push, and the body begins to roll back up.

When the hand reaches a point close to the body, between the chest and waist, it flips over (180°). Once the hand flips over and pushes past the waist, the swimmer moves into a supine position momentarily. During the power phase, so far, the body has rolled down and back up and is now on its way to the other side. The hand stays close to the body as it continues to push downward, past the thigh, the elbow straightening. This last part of the power phase, called the finish, pushes the body to the other side. Finish with thumb up and snap the hand into the recovery without hesitation, as quickly as possible.

Arm stroking drills

When teaching the backstroke arm pull, break it into small pieces and have the swimmer focus on one thing at a time. When working on the recovery, shut out thoughts about the kick and what the arm is doing in the power phase.

• Working on the lift: Ask swimmers to lie on the deck and lift one arm (with the thumb leading) from the thigh to a point perpendicular to the body; they then lower it back to the side.

Work on a straight and stretched lift. Most young swimmers do not lift at the correct angle and do not stretch their arm enough; often they lift out rather than up. When they are on the deck, you can easily give them a feel for just how much they need to maximize lift. When they hit 90°, gently grab the arm and stretch it for them.

• Swimmers can work on the lift in the water, but without moving, by hooking their toes onto the edge of the pool. Lift and stretch to 90°, then let the arm return to the side.

• The same drill, but going the lap: The swimmer works on the first half of the recovery. The arm stretches, the whole way up, but at 90° the arm hyper-stretches. The feet kick, but the swimmer thinks only about the lift. Also, because the swimmer has rolled to the side, so that the shoulder is out, the lift will be higher than if he or she had remained flat. As the hand lifts from the thigh, the palm faces the midline. If the swimmer rolls to the right side, the right shoulder submerges and the left shoulder surfaces. The palm faces the direction of the roll. So the arm lifts up, then returns to the thigh; the swimmer repeats this on the opposite side.

• Ask the swimmer to stretch the arm when it reaches a point perpendicular to the body. To accent this important point in the lift, ask him or her to hold the arm in this stretched position and kick a lap. Remember to work both the left and right sides equally.

• With paddles: Wearing paddles exaggerates a stroke's feel and makes a swimmer more aware of the effects of a movement. When isolating the backstroke recovery, the paddles effectively give a swimmer a visual reference. He or she can spot the hand slicing the air in line with the body and can spot the arm arching (180°) from thigh to catch. The body roll makes this 180° arc possible. The hand stays on its arced path and doesn't move off the line. The hand lifts in line with the body, palm flat, thumb leading. When the hand turns mid-recovery, the body rolls, following the arm to the other side.

• Fist drills give a swimmer an interesting feel for the stroke. Suddenly hand power is gone and the rest of the body has to compensate. To temporarily delete one essential part strengthens the other parts, as well as the whole stroke.

• Working on the arms without the legs: Swimmers cross the legs or tie them together with bands, so they can't kick. The feet are going to weigh more once crossed. To keep the feet from sinking, swimmers need to stretch their bodies from head to toe and squeeze their buttocks muscles. Pinching the buttocks keeps the feet in line with the rest of the body and close to the surface. Swimmers must practice this drill in a streamlined position in order for it to be effective; thus, stress stretching and squeezing at first, more than a particular distance.

For young age-group swimmers who are still trying to gain control of their bodies in the water, you can add a small float to the legs. Pull buoys also work fine, as far as keeping the legs up, but they change buoyancy, and young swimmers need to practice balancing with them.

• The one-arm drill gives the swimmer a feeling for how the roll from side to side works with one arm. The swimmer digs deep, rolls to one side, and pushes to the waist. Still on that side, he or she begins to roll upward. The hand flips over, and he or she pushes to the thigh and rolls to the other side. The swimmer does not move the other arm. He or she rolls back to the right side while recovering with the right arm. The one-arm motion is repeated, and the swimmer continues to roll to both sides at the appropriate time.

When rolling back to the stroking side, the swimmer is recovering. He or she hits the eleven o'clock again, digs deep, pushes to the waist, and starts rolling back up. The hand flips over and pushes to the thigh, and the swimmer rolls to the other side. This drill gives the student a feeling for how the body roll is timed with the power phase. Isolate one part to better understand it. Practice with the left arm only, too.

It's hard for age-group swimmers to do a one-arm-pull drill with a three-beat kick on each side, because they lose forward momentum without the other arm pull; thus, the timing of the arm stroke with kick is thrown off. If you want to give them a feel for how the power phase works with the roll and kick, try this drill with fins. With fins on, they can fit in three kicks per side.

Wearing fins factors the forward momentum back in. Thus, swimmers can practice with one arm without losing the timing of the whole stroke.

Timing

Kick and roll: The body rolls to the right as the right hand catches the water at the eleven o'clock. Flutter kick (1, 2, 3) on the right side: kick with right (1), then the left (2), then the right (3) foot. The swimmer rolls down on the first kick, moves slightly up on the second kick, and the third kick pushes him or her over to the other side. Thus, the third kick, the right foot, helps to drive the hips to the left so the swimmer can start the left kick on the left side.

The body rolls to the left as the left hand catches the water at the one o'clock. Flutter kick (1,2,3) on the left side: kick with the left (1), then the right (2), then the left (3) foot. Roll down (1), move slightly up (2), kick and roll (3).

The recovery and roll: The hand snaps upward from the thigh, thumb leading, and the body rolls to its deepest point on the side opposite the lifted arm (1); the hand reaches the 90° point, turns 180°, and the body rolls up, toward the lifted arm (2); the pinkie catches the water, and the body rolls with the arm toward the catch (3).

The power phase and roll: The hand slices through the water below the catch, and the body follows, rolling down (1); the hand pivots and pushes in toward the waist, and the body rolls back up (2); the hand flips over and pushes down past the thigh, and the body rolls onto the other side (3).

Right and left arm: The swimmer rolls to the right as the hand slices deep. Then he or she lifts the left arm as the right arm pushes in towards the waist.

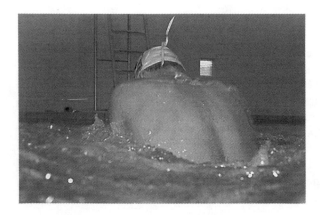

Breaststroke

Teaching the breaststroke

Children may join a swim team with no breaststroke experience, and you may have to teach this stroke from scratch; others will range in skill, no matter what their age. Because this stroke is complex, continually changing, and easily adapted into various styles (such as flat and wave), you can assume that all age-group swimmers need refining. When teaching the breaststroke, you want to start with the kick, move to the arms, and then to the coordination of the arms and legs in relation to the body.

The whip kick

The swimmer begins with the legs together and extended. First, he or she bends the knees and kicks the heels towards the buttocks. The closer to the buttocks, the larger the kick. A deeper, larger kick means a more powerful kick. Next, the lower legs circle around the knees while the upper legs remain *almost* stationary; the knees spread no farther than shoulder width. Going on the theory that a swimmer wants to be as compact as possible, moving outside of the body's widest point, the shoulders, will add width to the stroke and thus create additional drag. Thus, if the swimmer moves the upper legs too much, he or she gives up streamlining. To finish the kick, the legs squeeze together and stretch as the body glides. The stretch and glide are crucial.

The feet are flat when moving up towards the buttocks and then around the knees. Also, once the heel of the flat foot is close to the buttocks, the toes turn outward (like a duck). When the legs squeeze together and the swimmer stretches them and glides, the feet relax. Much power is generated from inside the leg and foot as they push together.

Teaching the kick

With some youngsters, the whip kick is a natural motion, while others need time to coordinate the movement. In order for the legs to move in this fashion, swimmers need to be flexible or develop flexibility by stretching regularly. Swimmers perform within their range of motion, which can grow as they grow if they incorporate stretching into their workout.

A few drills:

• Teach the breaststroke kick on the back (or from the elementary backstroke position). Students get use to bending their knees—rather than lifting them—and kicking down. When in a prone position, the concept is the same. The knees bend, but do not move up or down; the lower leg moves, heels leading a flat foot to the buttocks.

• Students stretch their arms along their sides, hooking their thumbs to the bottom edge of their bathing suits; next, they kick their heels to their hands. This can be done on both the front and the back, until they get use to kicking their heels towards their buttocks, moving the lower leg rather than the whole leg.

• While on the back, place barbells under the knees and move only the lower legs.

• Place a pull buoy or sponge ball between a swimmer's legs. The swimmer must hold the ball and thus cannot move his or her knees out too far—not without dropping the ball. This drill helps swimmers keep their knees in; use the lower part of the leg, which moves around the knees; and correct frog and scissors kick problems.

• The eggbeater works in the same way the whip kick does; the lower leg rotates around the knee. But instead of working both legs together, one leg mirroring the other, the legs alternate. Some children will have a natural eggbeater kick that you can then convert into a whip kick; others will have to work harder to learn the eggbeater, but can learn it with practice. Because the eggbeater and whip kick are similar, practicing one will aid the other. Swimmers can practice the eggbeater or whip kick vertically in the deep end. Ask them to do this with their hands out of the water for X number of minutes. Increase minutes with practice.

• In the deep end, swimmers execute feet-first surface dives to the bottom of the pool. Then they whip kick or eggbeater up to the surface. Repeat this ten times, without stopping. With practice, increase the amount of kick-ups, or time the exercise and try to go faster.

• Swimmers can work on a rotary (eggbeater) kick, in a prone position, with a board. They must hold their shoulders out of the water, so the feet don't break the surface. It's just another drill to work on the lower leg rotation around the knee—but alternately rather than at the same time. The drill aids coordination. The whip kick can also be practiced with a kickboard. Ask swimmers to focus on keeping their heads and spines in line while whip kicking.

• You can also have swimmers prone kick without a board, locking thumbs together and stretching the arms in the front of them. This takes more strength, for swimmers have to rely on their bodies and core control. This enables swimmers to work on the kick and changing body position at the same time, all the while keeping the spine and head in line.

• Ask swimmers to lie on the deck and execute the whip kick. Note that while on a flat plane the legs will break the surface, which will create drag. Thus, the kick begins at a depth, after the upper body has lifted.

• Swimmers can sit anywhere and practice turning both their feet out.

• They can stand on the deck with their feet pointed out. Not allowing the feet to move, they can squat (as far as possible) to the ground.

• Swimmers can also perform many in and out of the water exercises, both with flat feet and pointed toes, the purpose being to feel the difference between the two. Students can rotate their flat feet inward and outward to work on ankle flexibility.

The arm stroke

The elbows remain stationary, while just the forearms move—*out* from the streamline, then *in* to a prayer position under the chin, and *recovering* by returning to the streamline.

A swimmer needs to pay attention to the pitch of the hands throughout the pull. The hands need to be pitched at the angle where the swimmer gets the maximum amount of pull and push. Prone sculls that move head first, like the canoe and alligator, help breaststrokers get a feel for the role the pitch of the hands plays in pushing, pulling, and slicing the water. In propelling their bodies forward without their legs, they increase their hand power.

The outsweep: Swimmers begin from the streamline, with the backs of the hands together, thumbs down, pinkies up. They push the palms out, but not too far. The wider the pull, the more resistance. Remember, anything out of the streamline should add propulsion or lift; or, minimize movement out of the streamline. At this point in the arm pull, we are concerned with minimizing movement out of the streamline since lift and propulsion don't come into play until later. The body stays flat during the outsweep; movement up or down will cause the hips to sink or rise, which will increase resistance.

Insweep: The palms pivot, face the pool bottom, then shift again, slicing and pushing back under the elbows, which bend but stay on the surface. If the elbows sink, resistance increases. Also, the elbows remain in front of the shoulders' axis, for too long a pull will create drag. Next, the palms face inward, towards the middle of the body, and the inside of the arm pushes together and up. The palms meet in a prayer position, and may or may not be out of the water. This is the highest point of the lift, and a swimmer doesn't want to *try* to lift any higher once the hands meet here. Lift high and the force goes down; a swimmer wants to recover forward, not down. The hips move forward on the insweep, so the body is arched when the hands are in the prayer position.

The recovery begins with the hands joined in prayer under the chin. The swimmer stretches the arms forward, lunging toward the streamline position. He or she levels out while moving forward. At the end of the recovery, the whole body stretches, not just the arms and legs; the swimmer wants to get the maximum out of the glide. The position of the palms varies, and there

is no right or wrong. Some coaches advocate keeping the palms flat and under (but near) the surface; others teach palms together or up. As a swimmer, I personally like keeping the palms together throughout the recovery and flattening them out while streamlining.

While the arm stroke is now complete, it's important to consider where the lift and propulsive elements come in. The lift: As the hands pull through the water, pushing toward and under the elbows, the body moves forward and arches. By arching, the upper body lifts. The swimmer doesn't need to lift his or her head to take a breath, for the pull and arch work as one to naturally lift the head up.

Propulsion is greatest during recovery. From the arched, prayer position, the swimmer lunges forward and the shoulders rise, helping to reduce resistance. He or she levels out, stretching into the streamline. At the same time, the legs whip; thus, both arms and legs work in unison and propel the body forward. Driving the head while gliding increases momentum. Streamlining adds force to the motion that follows, which is the outsweep. Through hyperextending at the glide, the stretched arm when outsweeping pushes the water more forcefully. This is what I call the rubber band effect, or getting the most out of a movement. You stretch something, then let go, and an added force moves in the same direction as the movement being executed.

Considering speed: If the swimmer keeps the arms going, the legs will follow. Speed accelerates from the outsweep to the recovery; thus, the insweep is faster than the outsweep, and the recovery is even faster. The swimmer pulls, then falls fast. The minute the chin hits the water, the face and streamline follow.

Arm-stroke drills
Instructions to swimmers:
• Wear aqua fins with the butterfly insert, so the feet are locked. Practice a dolphin kick with a breaststroke pull to feel the wave-like motion and lunge over the wave to the glide.
• Work on faster arms by executing a breaststroke pull with the flutter kick. Even faster, flutter kick with zoomers.

• Execute a breaststroke pull with the legs crossed. Once crossed, the legs become heavy. To keep them on the surface, stretch the body and squeeze the buttocks. To compensate for the additional drag, the arms must be pitched correctly and must push the water more forcefully in order for the body to move forward.

This drill works in the same way a scull does. When in a prone position and canoe sculling, for example, the hands move in small circles on either side of the body, close to the shoulders. The synchronized swimmer will strive to maintain the foot on the surface, whether the head is raised or submerged. Alignment and core control are crucial if the body is to move forward fluidly.

Body position

The swimmer remains flat during the outsweep, lifts the upper body during the insweep, lunges forward during the recovery, and stretches at the glide, thus moving from a streamline to an arch to a streamline. The transition from one body position to another should be smooth rather than jerky. During all phases of the stroke, the body should be compact. At the end of the recovery, the swimmer stretches lengthwise as much as possible.

The arch position: When the swimmer begins the kick, his or her upper body has lifted, yet a straight line runs from the top of the head all the way down the back; thus, the head and back are in line, even though the body is in a kind of arch. The shoulders squeeze together, towards the center of the body, the palms praying. When the knees bend, so that the heels can move to the buttocks, the body is at an angle so that the feet won't break the surface. As the swimmer lunges forward, whipping, the body flattens out. Throughout the breaststroke, the head and spine are in line. Thus, when I use the word arch, I refer to the body position not the back, for the back itself is always straight and in line with the head.

Timing

In the breaststroke, the synchronization of the kick and the pull is critical and evolves from a lot of practice. To time this out, break the stroke into four counts. Count 1 and 2: The body moves from the streamline to the arch. The arms outsweep on 1, insweep on 2; the timing of the outsweep overlaps slightly, as the tempo increases with the insweep. The legs extend and glide on 1 and 2. Count 3 and 4: The body moves from the arch to the streamline. The arms recover on 3, accelerating, then stretch and glide on 4. Bend the knees and kick the heels to the buttocks on 3, and whip on 4.

Thus, you can see the alternating movement of the arms and legs, for the arms circle as the legs stretch and glide (1,2), and then the legs kick as the arms recover, stretching to a glide (3,4). The stresses fall on counts 2 and 4, as these counts incorporate the important components of lift, propulsion, and streamline. Count 2 equals the end of the insweep, when in the prayer position, prior to the lunge. In this position the body is compact and at the height of the lift. Count 4 equals the streamline, where the body meets the least resistance, and that streamline follows the whip kick and lunge, the most propulsive phase.

Freestyle

The universal stroke

Most swim teamers, no matter their age, will agree that they have thought about, and employed, the crawl stroke more than any other stroke. No doubt, the crawl stroke dominates most workouts. There are several reasons for this. The crawl stroke is the first stroke a youngster learns in a learn-to-swim program. An eight-and-under will know the crawl, but may or may not know the other strokes. Because the crawl is the easiest stroke on the muscles and joints, it is used early in the season, to get swimmers into shape, and it is used early in a workout, to warm swimmers up. Swimmers swim a lot of crawl throughout a season, because they can handle large amounts of it with less stress on the muscles and joints. When upping yardage, usually this means more crawl. At meets, the freestyle is the most popular and the most competitive of events. There are usually more heats of it, yet at the same time those who compete in freestyle events have to work harder to have an edge.

Body position

When teaching the crawl stroke, begin with the body position. The body must be balanced and streamlined in order for it to move effectively through the water. Neither the head nor the feet should be up or down. If the head is up (the most common scenario of the two), the feet will most likely be too deep. The body will not be streamlined, and frontal drag will hinder forward velocity. Less common is the swimmer whose head is too deep. I have seen two cases of this. In the first situation, the deep head caused the swimmer's whole body to sink below the surface. This made his arm stroke difficult. In the second situation, the deep head caused the feet to rise above the surface, and the swimmer was kicking the air rather than the water—and going nowhere.

As in all strokes, the swimmer wants to stretch and be as compact in width as possible. He or she keeps the body in line and uses the head—which looks down, not forward—as an anchor point. While a streamlined position may seem elementary, most youngsters have to work on this. Until the body is balanced, the swimmer will fight the water and make little forward progress.

As the swimmer moves through the water, he or she rolls the hips and shoulders as a unit from side to side. Keeping the head in line with the body, he or she rolls to one side with one arm stroke and to the other side with the other arm stroke. Instead of thinking about one arm at a time, he or she thinks about one side at a time, but without a pause between the two. The body roll allows the hands, while in contact with the water, to be pitched at the most effective angles. The roll adds force to both the catch and the finish. By rolling, the swimmer achieves maximum stroke length, for he or she can reach farther if the shoulder is tilted on its side. This is also the perfect spot to breathe, as no extra effort is needed to obtain the oxygen that will enable him or her to continue.

The flutter kick

The legs remain stretched and close to one another while they kick up and down from the hip, one at a time. The foot acts as a paddle, the top of the foot pushing the water one way and the bottom of the foot pushing the water the other way. While one foot pushes the water up, the other foot pushes the water down. If the foot is flat, it cannot push the water; thus, the toes must be pointed. The foot curves in slightly; the ankle is relaxed. The knees bend slightly on the downbeat and straighten on the upbeat. Too much of a bend in the knee (a bicycle action) creates drag. Eliminate the bicycle action by working with flippers.

The swimmer executes a small, quick kick close to the surface. The smaller the kick, the less drag. A large kick—kicking wide or deep—will create form drag and be slower. Remember streamlining principles: minimize movement out of the streamline; do not add any more width to a stroke than is necessary. The small, quick kick is closest to the streamline. Yet, take into consideration that a distance freestyler's kick will be slightly deeper than a sprinter's kick. Speed causes a swimmer to naturally ride higher in the water.

The kicking works in unison with the body roll. Three kicks on each side (or per arm stroke) or six kicks per stroke cycle is the most common and the most effective tempo.

Kicking drills

Kicking drills strengthen the legs. The stronger the legs the stronger the kick, and the stronger the kick the stronger the stroke. Approximately 30% of the crawl stroke's power comes from the kick. The swimmer wants to utilize that 30% to the fullest.

• Flutter kick while streamlining: The swimmer places the arms out front, one hand on top of the other. The upper arms squeeze the head behind the ears; the elbows press as close to one another as possible. The chin tucks to the chest, and the swimmer looks at the bottom of the pool while stretching.

• Flutter kick with a kickboard: With the board, a swimmer can kick hard without worrying about losing oxygen. More of his or her energy and concentration can be put into kicking. The swimmer should use a board that allows him or her to keep the shoulders in the water and to stay fairly close to the streamline.

• Flutter kick a lap on one side, and then a lap on the other side: The bottom arm leads, extending out front near the surface, while the top arm stays at your side. The swimmer works on a small, quick kick and on kicking both ways: up with the top of the foot and down with the bottom of the foot. The swimmer stretches and remains in line.

• Flutter kick longer than three beats per side: Drill 10, 8, 6, 4, and finally 3 (kicks) on each side, so swimmers get a feel for the kick and roll in relation to the power phase. Stress the three-beat kick per arm pull as the desired timing. Swimmers work on thrusting the hips and rolling in line.

• Flutter kicking with zoomers: This develops ankle flexibility, strengthens the legs, and raises the heart rate.

• Flutter kicking with aquafins: Aquafins work the quadriceps. They add weight to the legs, so the swimmer has to kick hard from the hips. They reinforce a small, quick kick, because it's difficult to execute a large kick with them on.

• Flutter kick short distances as hard as possible: Rest and repeat.

• Vertical kicks: This is done in the deep end to develop the leg muscles, as well as elevate the heart rate. Swimmers kick small and quick from the hips, the top part of the foot pushing the water one way and the bottom part of the foot pushing the water the other way.

• Execute the crawl stroke with the head up: This adds vertical resistance. The swimmer feels as though he or she is swimming against a wall. He or she has to work the arms harder to keep the momentum going forward. It takes strength to execute this drill, especially when adding yardage and intensity.

The arm stroke

The recovery begins with the arm stretched at the side, the palm facing the thigh. The hand exits the water, pinkie finger first, but with the elbow bending and leading the lift. The fingertips, which remain close to the surface throughout the recovery, trace a straight path from the exit point at the thigh to the catch point in front and in line with the shoulder. In order to make a straight line between these two points, the elbow must bend sharply as its lifts and points skyward, so that the forearm can travel under it and thus remain close to the body.

If the arm does not recover in line and close to the body, if the hand travels around the elbow instead of underneath it, a swimmer encounters drag. If the recovering arm is straight rather than bent, a swimmer will tire faster, for lifting the hand above the elbow is less economical, from an energy standpoint. A bent arm recovery offers the most direct path from the thigh to the catch. And the sharper and higher the elbow, the better.

Good swimmers look effortless. They relax the recovering arm. Imagine a puppet, and a string pulling up the elbow, but nothing else; the rest of the arm is loose and dangles. While the fingertips hang close to the surface, they never touch it (for then the swimmer encounters drag).

The same imaginary string that lifts the elbow also lowers it gradually, as the hand passes the ear and the forearm moves forward to the catch.

The hand catches the water in line with the shoulder, index finger first, hand pitched at a 45° angle. The swimmer stretches the arm (and the whole body) prior to and after the catch. The hand moves easier and quicker though air than water, so to catch the water too close to the head will slow the arm down as it meets the water's resistance. By rolling shoulder down with the stretching arm, more stroke length is attained and more force is applied to the power phase of the stroke. If the right hand catches, the right shoulder rolls down and the left shoulder rolls up. But you are not completely on your side. Rolling too far will slow forward movement.

While reaching with the arm and rolling the body, press down with the palm. The hand descends ten to twelve inches below the surface. Next, the palm presses towards the waist, drawing a straight line under the body. The elbow bends and remains elevated above the hand at this moment and throughout the power phase. After pressing straight to the waist, the hand follows the contour of the body and pushes past the hips. The thumb lightly brushes the thigh as the swimmer finishes the power phase by snapping the wrist. He or she sweeps the hand (pinkie first) up with the body roll at the finish. The shoulder rolls up with the recovering arm.

The swimmer wants to keep the power phase path in line and close to the body. The arm must move in line with the body, never traveling outside the widest part, which is the shoulder. The swimmer traces a straight line from the catch point to the finish point. The palm pushes along that line; the elbow bends so that the lower arm travels under it. The body roll adds force to the *press* (after the catch, as the body rolls down) and to the *push* (at the finish, as the body rolls up).

Coach's correction: head down,
eyes pointed to the pool bottom

Stroking drills

• Stroke with one arm: The other arm can be extended out in front or can be glued to the side. Either way, the swimmer can work on the recovery and the power phase as one fluid movement.

• Catch-up crawl: One arm recovers and is on its way to the catch while the other arm descends from the catch to a depth of approximately ten to twelve inches.

• Work on the power phase without the recovery: The swimmer rolls and reaches, then presses into the waist and pushes out at the thigh; he or she repeats this with the other arm. The arms never break the surface. The American Red Cross used to call this the Beginner Crawl.

• Fingertips, from the beginning to the end of the power phase, trace the the black line on the bottom of the pool.

• Fingertip drag: to exaggerate that the fingers stay below the elbow and close to the surface.

• Stretch a rope parallel to the wall and close enough in so that the swimmer will have to swim a tight (compact) stroke. The goal is to achieve a high elbow recovery.

• The use of the paddles will give a swimmer a feel for the way the palms need to be pitched during the power phase.

• Aquafins help young swimmers lift their elbows high, so that their fingertips stay above the water throughout the recovery. Aquafins add resistance to the power phase, increasing difficulty and thus building muscle, but at the same time free the palms, so the swimmer can still maintain a feel.

• With or without zoomers, the swimmer lies on his or her side with the underarm stretched out in front, above the head, and the upper arm glued to the side. The swimmer kicks six times, then rolls to the opposite side, where he or she switches arms. He or she repeats the motion from side to side—6 kicks on the right side, power pull with right arm while rolling to the left side, 6 kicks on the left side and power pull with the left arm.

Breathing

When a swimmer breathes properly, you can hardly tell that he or she is taking a breath. The head stays in line with the spine and rolls with the body, never independent of it. Just before rolling, the swimmer exhales all of the remaining air, so that when the mouth breaks the surface he or she can breathe in fresh air. He or she only needs a small, quick breath to keep going.

The swimmer can breathe to one or both sides. He or she can breathe every two, three, four, or more strokes. By setting a rhythm, the swimmer will not go into oxygen debt as easily. Most swimmers favor one side, but bilateral breathing—breathing to one side and then the other—is far superior.

Breathing after the third stroke sets a perfect rhythm, in that breathing after two strokes seems too often and breathing after four strokes seems too long. Breathing after three, rather than two, strokes is faster. The swimmer should be able to stretch his or her limit and add a stroke. Breathing after four strokes seems to lend itself to oxygen, and thus energy, depletion. While it is best to set up a rhythm when crawl stroking, when racing the swimmer may change it. For example, when sprinting, he or she may breathe less; when swimming a distance, he or she may breathe more.

Bilateral breathing allows a swimmer to roll evenly on both sides; the stroke becomes more balanced. When breathing to one side, the swimmer rolls more with that side of the body and pulls more with that arm. The other side of the body has equal potential, which isn't being used. Even if the swimmer rolls to the non-breathing side, it is doubtful that he or she is utilizing that roll to its fullest. By choosing to breathe bilaterally, the swimmer increases his or her power. Bilateral breathing also prevents an injury that may result from utilizing one side over another—especially in a swim team setting, where you are swimming a lot of yardage in a day and in a week.

Some people believe that bilateral breathing is more difficult than breathing to one side, but this is not true. The difficulty occurs when the swimmer has developed a one-side breathing habit and has to break it. But it's worth the time and work, for in the end the swimmer will have a more efficient stroke.

Swimmers who have spent years breathing to one side can practice side kicking on the non-breathing side on a daily basis. Divide the freestyle portion of the daily workout into: (1) bilateral breathing and (2) breathing on the non-breathing side only. Do not allow them to lapse back into breathing on the one side they have favored for so long. Increase the bilateral breathing laps; eventually every lap should be bilateral.

Breathing drills
   • Experiment with a variety of breathing rhythms: Swimmers breathe after every stroke cycle, then after every three, four, five, or six strokes.
   • Swim 25 yards fast, without breathing: While this drill will not make a swimmer swim faster, it will increase his or her cardiovascular endurance. The drill also gives a swimmer a feel for what it is like to experience oxygen debt. All swimmers should recognize the signals, so they can act (breathe sufficiently).
   • Crawl stroke with a snorkel: This builds up a swimmer's lung capacity and cardiovascular endurance. He or she can practice the body roll without the breathing.
   • Play games, like shark, where swimmers have to hold their breath.
   • Underwater dolphin kicking: This can be practiced with or without zoomers or monofins.

Timing
   The right arm catches (1), presses down (2), and presses to the waist (3). The right shoulder rolls down, and the swimmer kicks 1, 2, 3 on the right side. The left arm catches (4), presses down (5), and presses to the waist (6). The left shoulder rolls down, and the swimmer kicks 4, 5, 6 on the left side.

   On 4, the right arm pushes to the thigh, finishing the power phase; on 5, the recovery begins, and the swimmer can breathe; on 6, the fingertips pass the mouth as the head and belly roll down. On 1, the left arm pushes to the thigh, finishing the power phase; on 2, the recovery begins, and the swimmer can breathe; on 3, the fingertips pass the mouth as the head and belly roll down.

   Note that on the third count, the right arm presses towards the waist and the left hand passes the mouth. This catch-up phase of the stroke allows for continuous propulsion. This happens again on count 6, when the left arm presses to the waist and the right hand passes the mouth.

Starts

Take your mark / go

The more relaxed a swimmer is at the start, the better his or her performance will be. A swimmer needs to stay calm and loose while waiting for his or her heat. He or she can breathe slowly in and out; can stretch; and can shake the limbs. Three short whistles means move close to the diving platform. One long whistle means step onto the back of the block (for the freestyle, butterfly, or breaststroke). The deck referee signals to the starter. When the starter says, "Swimmers take your mark," the swimmer moves into either the grab or track position.

According to FINA starting procedures, at least one foot must be placed at the front of the starting platform, but there is no rule on how close or far apart the feet should be. In the grab position, both feet are placed next to one another at the front of the diving platform. The hands grab the block either in-between or outside of the feet. In the track position, one foot is placed

ahead of the other. The fastest reacting leg is placed to the rear, approximately mid-block. A swimmer determines the fastest reacting leg by falling forward and seeing which one catches the body.

In both positions, the hands hold the edge of the platform, and this stabilizes the body. Swimmers can also pull back on the block before launching forward and achieve added momentum. When swimmers take their mark, their bodies are crouched, their heads are down, and they look at their knees. On the *go* signal, they spring off the block and streamline. The arms move from the edge of the block straight out—never swinging back, only forward. Streamlining while in the air adds both length and speed to the dive, and thus is a great source of power.

After streamlining, swimmers must pike and target a point of entry. Visualize a hole in the water and a "slide" (Skinner) angled at 40° through that hole. The hands, head, shoulders, hips, and feet must travel through that hole and down that slide at a 40° angle. When the swimmer hits the hole right, he or she swishes into the water as though swishing down an actual slide; all momentum goes into the hole, and there is little splash.

When springing off the block, there are two potential velocities: horizontal (caused by leg

power) and vertical (caused by gravity). The potential for horizontal is greater than vertical, and the swimmer wants to maximize the available horizontal velocity. Yet he or she doesn't want to make the dive too long, for then gravity will come into play and drag will follow; he or she wants zero gravity when entering the hole. Getting a feel for where to target the point of entry takes practice, as well as clear communication between coach and athlete. While a coach can see when the athlete hits the hole right and when he or she doesn't, the athlete needs to be able to understand and feel the difference.

If any part of the body falls off the slide, the swimmer deals with both wave and form drag. Form drag results if the body doesn't move in line through the hole. Wave drag results when the part of the body that is not in line falls off the slide and slaps the water, creating turbulence. For example, the swimmer will slow down if he or she pulls his hands up too soon. The body will follow the hands and in doing so will not make it through the hole; the feet will slap the water. The swimmer needs to travel all the way down the slide before curving up.

Even if the hands, head, shoulders, and hips make it through the hole, the swimmer will slow down if the feet drop past the slide and slap the water. For example, those of us who learned the racing dive in the sixties have had to work on kicking up rather than dragging our legs, as we use to do. But "all things in moderation," for kicking up too high (not letting the legs slide through the hole at 40°) will cause the body to travel too deep and with maximum velocity. This can be slow, in that too much time is spent going down and then up rather than forward, and dangerous, depending on the water depth. The swimmer wants to direct the velocity in a horizontal rather than vertical direction.

At the bottom of the 40° slide, visualize a bowl. If the swimmer hits the slide right, he or she will curve off of it. He or she should be streamlining and will be traveling fast. When velocity begins to decrease, the swimmer begins dolphin kicking (in the butterfly, backstroke, and freestyle) or pulling out (in the breaststroke). If the swimmer breaks out of the streamline too soon, then he or she loses speed. If the swimmer holds the streamline too long (two body lengths), he or she also slows down and will lack momentum going into the next move. The swimmer wants to be one body length off the slide before breaking out.

The swimmer angles to the surface (moving forward and upward) gradually. He or she breaks the surface at or before fifteen meters. Once the swimmer breaks the surface, he or she doesn't need to take a breath, for the race has just begun, and there should be plenty of oxygen. He or she needs to get going. Later, the swimmer executes a normal breathing cycle, depending on the event he or she is swimming.

Practicing starts

Practicing starts will make swimmers faster. Focus first on refining technique, then on executing them fast. In practice, a coach should simulate the conditions swimmers face in competition and thus ready them.

• Swimmers should experiment with both the grab and track start, not just once, but enough to determine which one works best. They should practice stepping forward into the starting position upon hearing "swimmers take your mark."

• Practice control: holding the mark position for varying lengths of time. The swimmer wants to be in control of the mark position and not false start. No matter when the *go* signal occurs, the swimmer can react quickly.

• Practice fast reactions: Some swimmers are naturally quick with their reflexes; others have to develop this. How fast a swimmer responds to a beep, gun, or whistle and moves off the block needs to be practiced. Time their response; work on improving it.

• Teach starts through variations. Approach height is one variation. Practice step, step, dive from the poolside to work on getting momentum without the height of the block. On the block it's step, hold, dive. This drill helps the swimmer to put momentum into the streamline.

• The underwater dolphin kick has become one of the most efficient ways to move through the water, but only for those who have practiced it enough to develop that level of proficiency. First an age-group swimmer has to master the dolphin kick technique; then he or she must practice it enough to develop power, and must practice it fast in order to develop speed. Thus, underwater swimming should be incorporated into each workout. The swimmer can underwater dolphin kick on both the front (for butterfly and freestyle events) and the back (for backstroke event). Place a marker at fifteen meters, so swimmers can see the distance they are striving for.

The backstroke start

Swimmers enter the water after hearing a long blast. They get into position by grabbing the bar on the diving platform with both hands and positioning their feet underwater, right below the surface. On the signal "swimmers take your mark," they pull up to the bar, making space between the heels and thighs. When they hear the signal, they squeeze the rest of their body into the thighs. On the *go* signal, they push with the feet (up and out), lift the hips, and throw the arms and head back towards a streamlined position, arching the back in the process.

Watching this, you should see the body explode off the wall, and arch up and then down. Because the backstroker starts in the water rather than from a height, the back start has a greater potential for vertical velocity. The farther up out of the water the swimmer can get his or her body, the more horizontal velocity he or she can achieve

On the way down, the swimmer essentially targets the same hole and the same 40° slide, but has to travel through it backwards. The arms, head, shoulders, hips, and feet must travel through the hole and down the 40° slide. When the arms and head hit the hole, the body is arched. Each body part that follows snakes in the hole and straightens out once on the slide. Once the whole body is on the slide and then curving off, the swimmer streamlines and is traveling fast. At the crucial moment when velocity begins to decrease, he or she breaks out of the streamline and dolphin kicks. Gradually he or she angles to the surface, breaking at or before fifteen meters.

Turns and Finishes

Open turns

In an open turn, the swimmer swims into the wall, touches with one or two hands, and turns. In the freestyle and backstroke events, flip turns are preferred, because they are faster. But in the butterfly and breaststroke, the swimmer executes an open turn—with a two-hand touch. A swimmer will be disqualified if he or she flips.

The butterflier and breaststroker accelerate into the wall. When falling short of the wall, they streamline in, instead of taking an extra stroke. When the two hands touch "at, above, or below the surface" (USA 14), three things move at the same time: the legs, which tuck tightly under the body and move towards the wall; the head, which looks to the sky as it moves over the body, away from the wall; and the arm closest to the surface, which follows the head, brushing the ear as it moves into the streamline. The submerged arm sticks to the side during the reverse, but then moves into the streamline, joining the other arm. If either arm detours from its designated path, drag will result. The goal is to reverse quickly, and a swimmer does this by keeping the body compact. Also by accelerating into the wall, the swimmer will be faster off the wall.

After a swimmer executes the reverse, he or she plants both feet on the wall at a depth that is approximately 20% of his or her height. For example, a five-foot swimmer places both feet on the wall twelve inches below the surface. The minute the feet touch, the swimmer pushes off. He or she still wants to be in a tight tuck, for a tucked body will generate a more powerful push than a piked one. The swimmer pushes off the wall while on the back or side and turns onto the front while streamlining. He or she stays as horizontal as possible—not traveling deeper and not coming up right away. He or she does this to stay under the wave (caused by the swim into the wall), which eliminates drag.

When the swimmer feels the velocity from the push off begin to decrease, he or she either dolphin kicks (in the butterfly) or pulls out (in the breaststroke). He or she achieves maximum velocity with the push off and does not want to glide too long. Also, if the swimmer does not dolphin kick or pull out, if he or she just glides there, the turn will be significantly slower. The swimmer then angles (rather than pops) up to the surface, no more than fifteen meters from the wall.

The underwater dolphin kick

When swimming the butterfly, a swimmer turns and then can dolphin kick underwater up to fifteen meters; then he or she is required to surface. Many swimmers glide too long off their turns, and dolphin kicking when velocity begins to decrease is definitely faster than remaining in the glide while angling to the surface.

The event being preparing for and the need for oxygen throughout a race will help the swimmer determine how much time to spend swimming underwater after the push off. The swimmer may want to go the maximum distance, or he or she may want to assess the situation as something less than the maximum. For example, a distance swimmer wants to keep underwater swimming to a minimum, because going into oxygen debt will be detrimental to his or her performance. Distance swimmers need to set a pace and not trade oxygen debt for speed. While underwater dolphin kicking is fast, for some swimmers it is faster to surface before fifteen meters, even when sprinting. It's more important to focus on how fast, rather than how far, a swimmer can kick.

The pullout

When swimming the breaststroke, a swimmer reverses direction at the wall, pushes off from a tucked position, streamlines, and pulls out underwater once velocity begins to decrease and before angling up to the surface. Gliding off the turn and not pulling out is significantly slower. Also, the swimmer will lose speed if he or she glides for too long before pulling out.

Throughout the pull phase and recovery, the body remains chest down, with both shoulders parallel to the surface, so there is no question that the swimmer is on his or her front rather than side. The pullout begins from the streamline—one hand on top of the other, the thumb over the wrist, the elbows locked, and the upper arms squeezing the head behind the ears. The swimmer pulls out slightly beyond shoulder width, then down along the body—in at the waist and out at the thigh—so that the thumbs graze the hips and upper leg. The narrower the pull (the closer the hands are to the body), the less drag.

When pushing past the hips, the swimmer locks the elbows and squeezes the arms to the sides—but does not hold this position. Gliding at the end of the pull phase will slow a swimmer down. While the push off the wall generates velocity, and a swimmer can glide with it briefly (and that is productive), the velocity the pull generates is much less. Stopping there (to glide) is similar to stopping between the power phase and the recovery of any of the four strokes (something a swimmer doesn't do). The swimmer wants one continuous motion from the pull phase to the recovery. Otherwise, he or she experiences static rather than dynamic inertia when moving from one to the other. It's easier to move from an already moving state. Thus, the swimmer moves out of the pull phase and into the recovery without pause, but at the same time finishes off the pull phase by squeezing the arms to the side. The most powerful part of the pull phase is the finish.

The recovery begins when the thumbs leave the side of the body after the pull phase and move towards each other. The palms face the body as they pass under it. As the hands near one another, under the belly button, the fingertips turn in. One hand passes under the other as both hands cross, then continue to move in a crossed position, passing under the chin. The palms flip over, so they face the bottom of the pool as the swimmer streamlines. While the arms are recovering, the swimmer kicks and angles gradually to the surface, keeping the kick narrow, to eliminate drag.

The flip turn

When swimming the crawl stroke into the wall, the swimmer maintains speed and keeps the head down. The last arm to recover pulls to the thigh—which is where the other arm is positioned—as the swimmer presses the upper torso under the surface. As he or she flips, the two hands—positioned thumb in at the thigh—push past the body, adding momentum to the turn. The palms flip over as the body flips, so the hands can continue to push in the direction of the roll. Staying close to the body, the arms take the shortest path to the streamline.

Since pushing off the wall from a tuck generates more velocity than pushing off from a pike, the swimmer wants to swim in close enough so that after he or she executes a tucked flip the feet will touch the wall. When tucking, the head moves close to the knees; the chest presses to the thighs. The more compact the body the faster the transition from the last stroke (on the stomach) to the feet hitting the wall (on the back). When the two feet hit the wall at a depth that equals 20% of the swimmer's height, the swimmer is on his or her back and pushes off. The swimmer rotates to the side and (or) front, remaining as horizontal as possible to stay under the wave that has been caused by the body swimming into the wall.

When velocity begins to decrease, the swimmer dolphin kicks and angles to the surface, breaking it before or at the fifteen meter mark. While he or she can opt to use a flutter rather than dolphin kick while underwater, the flutter kick is significantly slower. Yet once on the surface, the swimmer must execute a flutter kick. Work on a smooth transition from the dolphin to flutter kick, and also a smooth transition from underwater to surface swimming. Breaking the surface on the side, shoulder and head at the same time, helps to prevent popping out of the water.

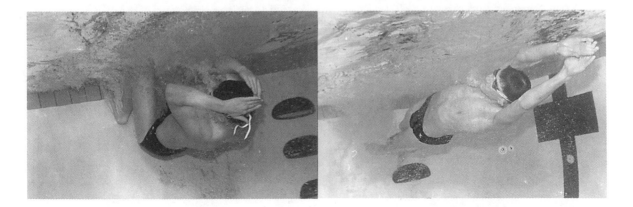

The backstroke flip turn

The backstroke flip turn is similar to the front-flip turn, with the difference being that the swimmer travels into and off of the wall on the back instead of the front. To begin with, string the backstroke flags up at practice, so swimmers learn how to use them. They will depend on the flags when executing their turns accurately in a meet. Teach your swimmers how to count their strokes from the flag to the wall. In the backstroke, it is especially important that swimmers learn to turn on both sides. They also need to be able to roll and flip with or without the arm stroke.

When backstroking into the wall, the swimmer rolls onto the front to execute the flip. Although the swimmer wants to base the timing of the roll and flip on the flags and the stroke count, he or she has to be prepared for error in a meet. One reason for error is that in practice or when warming up at a meet, swimmers may not swim into the wall as fast as they do when they are racing. This can throw their stroke count off. But with meet experience, swim teamers should have an accurate idea of their stroke count from the flag to the wall.

Troubleshooting: When backstroking, the head rolls in line with the body, and to move the head out of alignment will create drag; thus, looking for the wall will slow a swimmer down. But after counting strokes past the flags, he or she can roll and should know (without moving the head) if the wall is there. If the stroke count is off and a swimmer is too far from the wall, he or she has several choices: 1) power kicking on the back, then stretching while rolling; 2) rolling to the other side and flipping there; 3) taking one stroke on the stomach after the turn—if that hasn't been calculated in already. If the swimmer gears the stroke count for a tuck turn, which is more powerful, he or she can execute a pike turn if the wall is too far away. If the swimmer is a little close to the wall, he or she can flip without taking a stroke.

Whatever happens, the swimmer has many choices, but only one crucial moment. The USA Swimming rulebook states that "once the body has left the position on the back, there shall be no kick or arm pull that is independent of the continuous turning action" (15). Swimmers can prepare for competition by flipping at the wall when backstroking during practice. In practice the swimmer will experience all of these scenarios, repeatedly, and responding to them will become second nature. The goal is to apply full force to the turn and achieve one continuous, fluid motion.

After flipping and pushing off, the swimmer remains on the back and streamlines horizontally off the wall, staying under the wave. When velocity begins to decrease, he or she dolphin kicks on the back. Make sure swimmers remain in a tight streamline and keep their heads in line with their bodies. If the swimmer lifts the head while under the water, he or she will pop up rather than angle to the surface; when the raised head meets the resistance of the water, frontal drag results. Young swimmers commonly lift their heads—to keep water out of their noses. But it's crucial that they learn to blow out their nose from the wall to the point where they surface. You can drill them on this, and they will learn.

Teaching turns

When teaching turns, focus on technique first. Make sure that your swimmers are executing the turns correctly and working on the fine details; then focus on speed. Swimmers must practice racing turns every time they swim into a wall, not just during the portion of the workout designed for turns. Swimmers also need to practice accelerating into the wall, so that this will come naturally to them in a meet.

Once age-group swimmers learn the front and back flip turn, do not let them execute open turns in practice. Open turns allow them more rather than less oxygen. If they get use to this, even when they convert to a flip turn, they will slow down at the wall for that accustomed rest and extra oxygen. You want your swimmers to accelerate into the wall; you do not want them to grab extra breaths there. They can find all the oxygen they need during the lap itself, when stroking.

A few turn drills:

• To work on an open turn, swimmers place their two hands on the wall and prone float. At the sound of a whistle or a coach saying "go," they reverse, plant their feet on the wall, and push off. If swimmers can generate a fast turn from a stationary position, they will be fast when swimming into the wall.

• When first teaching the flip turn to youngsters, work in the shallow end on a front tuck. Focus on form—being compact, with the legs side by side and the head pressed to the knees. Help beginners find their balance when in a tucked position and maintain core control throughout the turn. Staying on a circular path, rather than tilting or falling to one side, will depend on the head position and on staying centered when leaning into the turn.

• To continue working on the flip, swimmers start at the wall, swim to the middle of the pool, and then execute a quick half-tuck. They keep the head down, and just before tucking, press the upper torso under the surface. This drill helps young swimmers who may be scared to swim fast into the wall work on swimming fast into the flip.

• Swimmers push off and streamline (without kicking) to a particular buoy on the lane line. Move the buoy and stretch farther. The focus here is on developing a more powerful push off the wall and on getting the most out of the streamline—by staying tight and by stretching.

• Swimmers try the same drill, but this time they break into the dolphin kick just before velocity decreases. Ask swimmers to feel for a change in velocity and think about where the breakout point needs to be. While a coach can be a swimmer's eyes, the swimmer is the only one who can feel what is happening.

• To work further on the push off, swimmers stand in the shallow end and jump up as high as they can. Drill them each day, repeating and increasing the jumps, but not letting the quantity of jumps outweigh the power they are trying to accomplish with each jump.

Fast turns

- Accelerate into the wall, and you will be faster off the wall.

- Swim into and off the wall on the same invisible line, as straight as possible.

- Stay compact: tuck tight and keep the arms close to the body.

- Push off from a depth that is 20% of your height. Stay under the wave, to avoid drag.

- Quick hands (open turns) or feet (flip turns). Touch and go.

- Streamline to maximize push-off speed.

- Dolphin kick or pull out when velocity decreases.

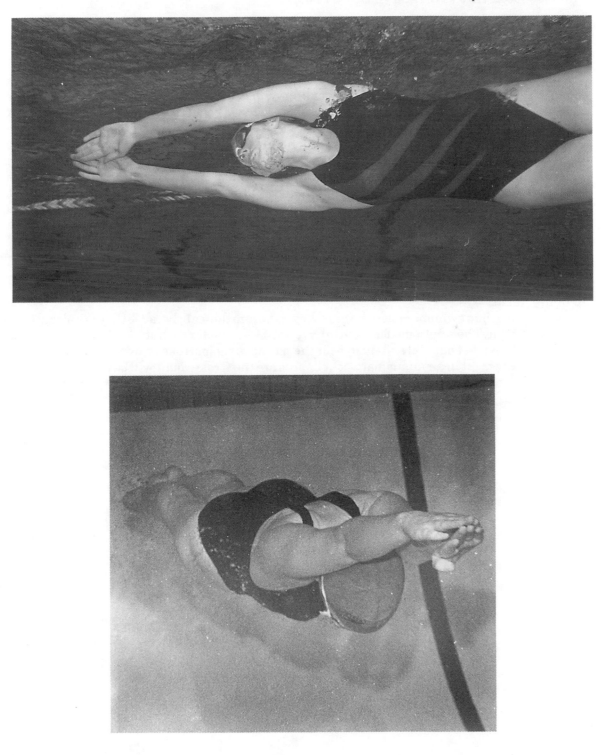

The finish

The finish is a crucial point in a race that is often overlooked and not worked on enough in practice—not as much as starts and turns. There are several reasons why age-group swimmers don't finish well when racing, and all of it boils down to training. If they run out of oxygen, they have not paced themselves adequately for the distance they need to achieve, have given too much too soon. If a backstroker is dying at the flags, it's going to be difficult to finish hard when the limbs struggle to make it to the end. Every racer needs a strategy for the event they are tackling. If they have trained well for the event and have a strategy, they should be able to finish strong.

A swimmer will also slow down coming into the finish if he or she looks for, rather than feels for, the wall. In the backstroke, rather than looking over the shoulder and throwing the head out of line, the swimmer counts strokes from the flags and powers into the wall. In the crawl, the swimmer keeps the head down going into the finish. The swimmer doesn't need to look for the wall, because the black cross on the bottom of the pool signals that he or she is only a stroke or two away. And when the swimmer executes a front flip turn with the head down and then does another with the head up, he or she can feel the difference. In a race, taking the time to look for the wall will cost the swimmer a couple of crucial seconds. Thus, technique is important, right up to the finish.

Some age-group swimmers slow down as they come into the wall, because they are afraid they are going to hit it. The solution is for them to have a stroke count for each stroke. Count in practice enough for this to feel natural and enough for them to have their stroke count memorized. If they attend an away meet in an unfamiliar pool, chances are the stroke count will be the same, as long as the pool sizes are the same. They can confirm this when warming up before the competition.

Train your swimmers to speed up (not slow down) when swimming into the wall. Slowing down is common, because this is what they will do in practice if the coach allows them to. Often

swimmers try to quit early; they glide into the wall. And since a coach has only one set of eyes and many swimmers to watch, this little detail may be overlooked when compared to what is happening in the middle of the pool. It is understandable that a coach will be watching strokes and have his or her hands full.

Often traveling into and off of the wall is used as a resting rather than an acceleration spot. What swimmers practice becomes a habit, and habits are hard to break. If you allow your swimmers to glide into their finishes at practice, chances are they will lack the experience to finish fast and solidly in a race. Make swimmers count their strokes and swim hard into the wall. Shoot for a definite touch, a strong ending to a good swim. Make the ending as important as the beginning and everything in-between.

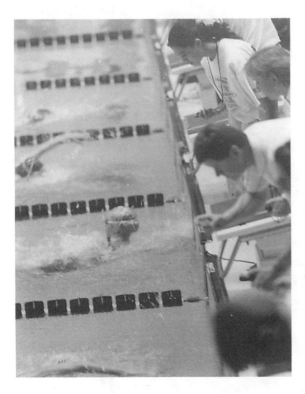

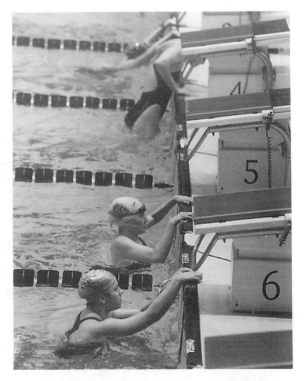

PART FIVE

Workout Components

The first plunge

When a swimmer first enters the pool, he or she feels a 15-20° temperature difference— the difference between the normal body temperature (98.6°) and pool temperatures (ranging from 78-84°). Some swimmers hesitate to take that first plunge. While the initial shock is physical, I believe some of it is mental. Momentarily, the first plunge constricts blood vessels, reduces circulation, and increases lactic acid. But the body acclimates to the lower temperature by the end of the first lap.

Warmup

When the body is at rest, the muscles are cold and stiff; when the body begins to move, the cold muscles initially resist. To move these cold muscles too quickly may cause muscle pulls and strains. Swimmers need to begin their workout slowly and work their way up to a faster pace gradually. This allows their muscles to warm up, literally. The warm-up portion of a workout increases the heart rate and breathing; makes the blood flow to the muscle tissues; which in turn raises the temperature of the muscles; which in turn loosens them, as well as the joints. Once the muscles are warm and loose, the swimmer is ready to increase the pace of the swim.

The swimmer warms up by swimming at a steady pace, either continuously or with short rests. The better conditioned he or she is, the tighter the muscles, and the longer it takes to loosen them. Thus, a coach may begin a season with a ten-minute warmup, and as the season progresses, increase to fifteen minutes. A conditioned swimmer typically warms up with a four- to five-hundred yard or meter swim, which should take from ten to fifteen minutes. Warming up for longer than fifteen minutes is wasted effort.

Once an age-group swimmer warms up, he or she must move into the workout. If the swimmer stops exercising for as long as fifteen minutes, he or she will have to warm up all over again.

Stretching

Follow the warmup with stretching exercises to further prepare the swimmer for activities-to-come. Stretching should always be done after the warmup, when the muscles are more pliable. Stretching after the warmup and before a vigorous workout 1) further loosens muscles; 2) develops flexibility, which will enable swimmers to execute parts of strokes with more efficiency and less chance of injury; 3) reduces a swimmer's chance of injury, not only by increasing his or her range of motion, but also by reducing muscle tension and soreness. A swimmer will be more flexible if he or she warms up and stretches regularly and properly. Thus, make these two activities a daily part of the workout. Five to ten minutes of stretching should be adequate.

When stretching, swimmers need to do a variety of exercises, striving to hit each muscle group. Secondly, they must stretch slowly. Rapid stretching causes unnecessary muscle tension and does not allow the swimmer to receive the full benefit of each exercise. Each exercise addresses a certain muscle or muscle group, and it is important to hold the stretch before moving on to the next exercise. Thirdly, swimmers need to stretch to the point where they feel the muscles being addressed, but not to the point of pain.

Finally, they must line up their bodies properly to get the full benefit of the stretch. For example, a swimmer stands on one leg in the shallow end, facing the wall. The other leg is raised perpendicular to the body, at a 90° angle; the foot rests on the edge of the deck. Before the swimmer even begins to move, make sure his or her two legs are straight. Make sure that the swimmer's shoulders and hips squarely face the wall, that the back is straight, and that the head is in line with the spine. Emphasize the importance of maintaining alignment as the swimmer leans chest down, towards the elevated leg. If a swimmer's back hunches, if the head drops, or if the knees bend, the stretch is ineffective. It is more important for the swimmer to execute this move in line than it is to see how close he or she can move the chest to the leg. The point is not to see how close the chest can move to the leg, but to stretch until the swimmer feels the stretch, but not beyond that to the point of pain.

Swimmers can stretch either in or out of the water. Whether on deck or in the water, the coach should choose, the swimmers should participate as a group, and the activity should be structured. If they stay in the water, have them exercise in a level area in the shallow end. If they stretch on deck, you can follow or incorporate into the stretching some stroke principles that may be harder to teach in the water.

Swimmers may complain about getting out of the pool after a warmup. Climbing out when wet may make them feel cold temporarily, depending on the air temperature, but they also know that later in the workout they will be heated. What follows the warmup is movement, both on the deck and in the water. Temperature changes are minor. If swimmers want to be tough, both physically and mentally, they have to tune out minor inconveniences and look to the overall good of what they are doing. It always helps for a coach to explain the benefits of an activity to his or her swimmers.

Sets

Every workout has a warmup and cooldown. In between the two, there are a variety of sets that need to touch each level of a swimmer's capability. When designing these sets, you want to consider how much time you have per workout. For example, you are teaching swimmers ages nine through twelve. They practice one hour per day, five days per week. It will take them at least ten minutes to warm up, ten minutes to cool down. Add five minutes of stretching, and you've used up twenty-five minutes. You only have thirty-five minutes for sets. You can fit in three, ten-minute sets, with five minutes left over for talking. You can see that one hour keeps both coach and swimmer moving.

Sets should:

• teach, so that coach and swimmer never lose sight of technique. There should be some detail at each practice that the swimmer is trying to refine. It may be a new concept, or a familiar one that the swimmer hasn't mastered yet. The teaching set is usually done at a low intensity.

• touch on each body part; work on the arms and legs, as well as on core control and core movements.

• be a combination of low, medium, and high intensity swims, depending on the time of the season, the distance of the swim, and the duration of the rest. When considering intensity, you consider heart rate. Vary the intensity not only within one workout, but also within one week. For example, if your swimmers swim five days a week, you may want to work them hard three of those days and easy two of those days; they also have the weekend to recover.

Rest

During swim-team practice, the rest is just as important as the swim time. Alternating work and rest increases the condition of the athlete. Resting during a workout enables a swimmer: 1) to recuperate from the previous swim, and the higher the intensity of the swim, the greater the need for rest; 2) to acquire oxygen and clear lactic acid from the muscles; 3) to gather in, rather than use up, energy; this readies him or her for the next swim. With a rest, the next swim can be a quality swim. Without a rest, a swimmer's stroke breaks down, as he or she gets tired. To continue to swim with a broken-down stroke is detrimental to the swimmer's technical progress.

Cooldown

Swimmers need to end their workout with a cooldown. This is a slow, easy swim followed by a few stretches. During this swim, the body cools gradually and gets rid of the lactic acid and other wastes accumulated in the muscle tissue during the workout. The heart rate drops slowly; natural circulation is restored. Stretching relaxes the muscles and reduces stiffness and soreness that can follow a hard workout. The swimmer who cools down will recover more quickly and be ready for the next workout.

If a swimmer does not cool down, and he or she enters the next workout tired and sore, over-training symptoms will occur, which will lead to staleness. To swim hard and then to stop abruptly is not good for the body. The muscles are warm, even hot, after a workout. To stop suddenly shocks even the most conditioned swimmer.

Training Factors

How a swimmer trains depends on a number of factors:

The type of season

There are two competitive seasons: short course and long course. Short-course meets are held in yard pools, and long-course meets are held in meter pools. If you are running a year-long, swim-team program, consider dividing your year into two separate training periods: short course, beginning in September and ending in February; and long course, beginning in March and ending in August.

The time of the season

Divide each six-month training period into three parts: early-season, mid-season, and late-season. Allow two months for each these.

Early season: Build an aerobic base to sustain an athlete through the six-month period. Visualize the base of a pyramid. You are conditioning the athlete; you are building endurance with distance swims and small rest cycles. Focus on teaching and learning. Each practice should be loaded with information and important activity. Swimmers should be learning proper stroke technique while they get into shape with predominantly freestyle workouts. Begin with the freestyle, for it is the most effective stroke to use when conditioning. Gradually add in the other strokes, beginning with the backstroke. Learning proper techniques is vital to swimmers doing well in competition later in the season. Also set aside time during each practice to work aggressively on starts and turns.

Mid-season: Visualize the pyramid growing taller, its sides narrowing; both of these things occur simultaneously, but gradually. The aerobic base is built, so now you focus on building up, not out. The volume, duration, and intensity of the work increases—but always (and importantly) gradually. Distance work decreases (in terms of workout percentage) while easy speed begins. Easy speed refers to 1) shorter swims with longer rest cycles; 2) whether the swim is done at 60%, 70%, 80%, etc. of the swimmer's heart rate. As the mid-season progresses, rest cycles are continually adapted to fit the swimmer's increasing capacity. It takes eight to twelve weeks for a swimmer to get into shape; thus, he or she starts to feel good in the middle of mid-season. Rest cycles grow shorter between sprints, and longer between distance swims. The coach and swimmer need to remain focused on technique, need to continue to work on all four strokes, starts, and turns. With starts and turns, swimmers should be focusing on tight streamlines and hard push-offs.

Late season: Continue to fine-tune strokes, starts, and turns. During the first two weeks of the late season, continue to increase volume, duration, and intensity. During the following four weeks, begin to gradually decrease the volume of the workout, but increase the intensity. During the final two weeks, hold the volume, but gradually decrease the intensity.

Championship meets are held late in a season. The goal is to peak during this time. A swimmer should peak two weeks into the late season. To peak means to perform at your highest level. Once a swimmer has pushed his or her body to its peak, he or she can only hold on to this state for six to eight weeks. Then the body de-conditions, because the intense workouts have zapped its strength. Recovery from hard swims and hard days takes longer. The swimmer cannot physically continue to work out at that high level. Just about the time the six-month season ends, the body sends a clear message that it is time to cut back.

Taper is done at the end of the season, prior to a big meet. Yardage decreases, but not enough for the swimmer to lose conditioning. More easy days are built into a week, to allow the body to regenerate. Swimmers taper to hold their peak state and to store energy for the coming meet. In striving to achieve the benefit of taper, they must limit participation not only in swimming, but also in other activities. Then swimmers enter the meet rested, with a high level of energy. This should lead to peak performance.

While many believe that age-group swimmers under the age of twelve do not need to taper, I believe in it, no matter what the age, because: 1) setting this up in the early years instills proper training habits and prepares a swimmer for the future; 2) some age-group swimmers stop swimming after a six-month season. Some will return after a break; some will not. It is healthier to ease them out of the sport gradually than all at once.

The length of the training time

If you cannot follow the six-month plan, you must determine the length of your training time. This, of course, follows targeting specific goals. Look at training in chunks; train within a block of time. Then divide that time into steps on a ladder, saving the last couple of weeks for taper. When building, ease swimmers into it gradually. You want them to be able to handle the increases. Always give swimmers adequate training time, so they are prepared to meet their goals. For example, one month will not prepare a swimmer for a championship meet. The solution is not to attend that meet; shoot for another.

Target competitions one by one. Some meets are bigger and more important than others. In a training program, shoot for the large meets and use the small meets as stepping-stones, for the more meet experience a swimmer has the better competitor he or she will be. Thus, you need the small meets to build up to the big one.

Think specifically. If a swimmer is just there to be there, swimming for all meets in the future, he or she probably isn't going to push as hard. Live for the immediately goal. Deal with the future in the future. Chances are that once you reach your immediate goal, your vision of the future will change anyway, for living involves learning, especially for age-group swimmers. To think of this as a non-ending activity is just too overwhelming and de-emphasizes the importance of the immediate season and goal. But if you have a specific goal you are working for and train for that event, then chances are you will be ready for it, come what may.

The time of day

Some swimmers don't have a choice as to what time of day to work out. Practice occurs at a certain time (maybe once, maybe twice a day). Typically, during the school year, age-group swimmers practice in the late afternoon, between school release and dinner hour. And that makes sense too, for after sitting in school all day, what better thing to do but exercise.

During the school year, swimmers usually compete on weekend mornings. Most USA Swimming meets begin with warm-ups at 8-8:30 p.m. and are finished by 2-3:00 p.m. The time of day in which swimmers practice usually differs from the time of day in which swimmers compete. Thus, coaches may want to consider an occasional morning workout, say on a Saturday when there isn't a meet. This instills flexibility into a swimmer, helps him or her to be more comfortable with the uncomfortable, or the unusual. This prepares the swimmer for competition, which is not the everyday occurrence. In the summer, workouts and meets can be held at any time of the day.

The pool

The size of the pool in which a swimmer trains affects his or her performance. A swimmer can train in a yard or meter pool for a short- or long-course meet. Those who practice in a longer pool have an advantage over those who work out in a short pool and compete in a longer pool. But for many swimmers, pool size may be "an uncontrollable" (Goldburg).

If you can control the water temperature, the optimum is colder. In 82° water, pulse rate will be five percent higher than in 80° water. Swimming in warm water increases red cell mass. If swimmers are not hydrating in 86° water, they will be hurt (Skinner).

The swimmer

I have talked in previous chapters about how individuals learn in different ways. You can teach two swimmers of the same age and skill level, and because they are individuals, they respond differently. Thus, age, skill level, and individuality must be considered in a training program. While you may lay out your season in an early-, mid-, and late-season pattern, you will require more of your older, advanced swimmers. Thus, designing a season will require more than one set of plans. Often, you will have three sets: one for eight-and-unders, one for swimmers ages nine through twelve, and one for swimmers ages thirteen and older.

Physiology

Anyone can enjoy swimming, refine technique, work hard, improve, and reach his or her potential, with years of dedication. All of this simply takes a love for swimming and a desire to master it. But not everyone can win the Olympics; on the elite level, physiology plays an important role. Certain body types do have an advantage over others in particular strokes and events. For example, tall, thin swimmers with long arms and legs have an advantage when sprinting in the backstroke and crawl. Or buoyancy is a necessary ingredient for a distance swimmer.

While physiology is an important consideration for an elite swimmer, for an age-grouper it is not. The goal is not to win or lose the Olympics, nor should it be to win or lose a race. The goal should be to apply full effort and to become the best that he or she can be, which takes years of commitment and training. Only then can a swimmer know what he or she is really capable of. Age-group swimmers need to focus on doing the most they can with the bodies that they have. Those who are the most technically advanced will have an advantage; and this especially applies to age-group swimmers.

While you want age-group swimmers to be versatile, you do want to take into account their potential in terms of a particular stroke or event. If a swimmer is buoyant, has good freestyle technique, and likes to swim distance, you certainly want to encourage that—but not at the exclusion of other strokes or events. One stroke effectively cross-trains a swimmer for another stroke. And within the spectrum of possible strokes and events in competition, all body types fit in somewhere. Thus, whatever a swimmer's size or shape, there is something at the end of the age-group road—if he or she wants to take it that far—that he or she can excel at in a big way.

The maintenance phase

Because of reversibility, it is important for coaches to educate age-group swimmers on how to maintain their aerobic base when they take breaks from swim team. Reversibility occurs when athletes take long vacations from exercise, and it particularly applies to swimming. When a swimmer stops swimming, the muscles shrink, and he or she loses strength and endurance. The muscles "lose their ability to utilize oxygen efficiently if they are not stressed constantly" (Mirkin and Hoffman 11).

If a swimmer swims all year, a few days out of the water, or one week, is no big deal. But after two to four weeks, a swimmer starts to lose all he or she has worked for. This doesn't mean that once back in the water on a regular basis that he or she can't gain it back with hard work, but it does mean starting all over again. Stopping and starting are counterproductive. It's better to continue to work out, even if the level of commitment changes. There are two reasons to prefer maintenance over stopping and starting: 1) Maintenance is easier on and better for the body. 2) Those who maintained begin the next season shifting into second gear; those who have stopped have to turn on the key, let the engine warm up, and then shift into first gear. They are in a catch-up position.

The maintenance phase is important for all competitive swimmers who do not swim all year round. Typically, age-group swimmers do other things besides swimming. Some commit to a part of, rather than a whole year. They may play other sports, for example. Crystal swims short course, from September through February, and then takes a break from swim team to play softball. She returns to swim team in the summer. Chelsea plays soccer during the fall, then joins swim team after that, in early November. When soccer starts up again in the spring, she does both. In the summer, she takes a break from organized sports altogether. Thus, she swims competitively for six months of the year. Many age-groupers swim the short-course season each year, and that's it. Some just swim in the summer, and that's it.

While the swim season is available in many places all year round, only a certain number of youngsters will want to be involved in that way. It may be expecting too much of children that they focus so intently on one thing at a young age. Having other interests gives their life a balance and can also help them to stay interested in swimming. After a break, they return eagerly.

A coach wants to give swimmers—who leave every fall to play soccer or every spring to play baseball—a training program, so they can maintain their aerobic base. They've spent a lot of time building it up, and rather than losing it completely, they hold on to what they have. Participation in other sports, while it may be good for a swimmer both physically and mentally, cannot replace swimming. The swimmer will lose the base and have to start all over again unless maintenance is done strictly in the swimming mode.

During the maintenance phase, a swimmer continues to swim, but at an easy pace, with a few short rests. He or she also cuts the workload in half. So if he or she swims on the team and workouts are held five days per week for one hour, during the maintenance phase, cut this in half: three, forty-five-minute workouts per week.

Case study #29

Kelly, a seventeen-year-old, swims all year round. But she spends six months in a maintenance phase and six months in a competitive phase. Her overall goal is competitive, but during the school year she is involved in so many school activities that it is harder for her to find the time to work out. She swims on the team from April-September and maintains her aerobic base from October-March.

During the competitive months she trains eight times per week. A workout ranges from one-and-a-half to three hours, or consists of a minimum of 4,000 yards. During the maintenance phase, she cuts the volume, duration, and intensity of her swims in half. She practices four times per week, alternating between one-and-a-half and two hours per day. This seven hours per week is enough to keep her aerobic base in check. She thinks in terms of time spent in the water, because time is what prevents her from swimming more. She gives the most she can to what she loves, while still fulfilling other obligations. She swims long distance with short rests, alternating strokes. Two-hundreds are common. She relaxes, enjoys the swims, and spends time thinking about technique, as well as trying out new ideas.

Training Concepts

Energy systems

Coaches speak in more than one language, and this becomes most obvious when they are talking about energy systems and training zones. I find the Australian Institute of Sport classification system straightforward and easy to understand. An athlete draws on both the aerobic and anaerobic energy systems when exercising. These systems can be broken down into various subsystems and training zones: A1 (low intensity, 65-75%), A2 (aerobic maintenance, 75-80%), A3 (aerobic development, 80-85%), AT (anaerobic threshold, 85-92%), MVO2 (maximal aerobic, 92-100%), and SP (sprint, 100%). I like focusing on the percentage of swim intensity, because I can apply this to my age-group swimmers as well as to my own training program. All ages can be working from the same page, and yet our pulse rates will be quite different.

Training in the aerobic system (while oxygen is present) builds endurance, removes lactic acid, and prepares the swimmer for anaerobic training. In the A1 zone, swimmers train at warm-up and cool-down pace, taking short rests; in the A2 zone, intensity and rest increase slightly. Training in both zones, over time, results in the development of an aerobic base, something that every swimmer needs before moving on to higher intensity training. In the A3 zone, swimmers develop their ability to utilize oxygen while further increasing intensity and rest.

In the AT zone, the transition between the aerobic and anaerobic systems, the swimmer achieves a pace where the production and removal of lactate in the blood is equal. Thus, the swimmer can determine maximum speed without lactate accumulation, which in turn determines his or her aerobic endurance.

Training in the anaerobic system increases speed and maximum endurance, and enhances lactate tolerance. In the MVO2 zone, swimmers exert approximately 90% effort with short swims and adequate rests to increase speed and maximum endurance. And lastly, you have the SP zone—going all out. When training in the anaerobic system, the swimmer exceeds his or her maximum oxygen uptake and accumulates lactic acid in the bloodstream. The swimmer can only sustain this system for so long before he or she has to move back into the aerobic system, where oxygen is available.

Lactic Acid

When the body is working, lactic acid is produced; thus, swimmers tolerate lactic acid in their muscles every time they swim. But at a certain point, lactate accumulates, and tolerance turns to pain. Symptoms of lactic-acid accumulation: the muscles hurt, cramp, are difficult to move, and the swimmer feels fatigued. First aid: easy swims, stretching, warm showers, massage, and rest.

Lactate-tolerance level varies from individual to individual, and also depends on how conditioned that individual is. When training regularly, a swimmer's aerobic capacity increases, which means the swimmer can process increasing amounts of oxygen; the anaerobic threshold rises. Maximum oxygen uptake refers to the maximum amount of oxygen that a particular swimmer's body takes in. This oxygen is then delivered to and used by the muscles. An athlete exercises comfortably at his or her maximum oxygen uptake level. As the athlete becomes more fit, this level rises.

Considering training zones for age-group swimmers

When considering training zones for age-group swimmers, it helps to break them down into two to three groups: eight-and-unders, twelve-and-unders, and those over thirteen. You need two to three sets of plans when training these groups.

Twelve-and-unders should 1) train in the aerobic system and fully develop their aerobic capacity; 2) develop good stroke, start, and turn technique. While young swimmers are growing, they may not have the ability to coordinate or intellectualize a stroke in terms of mastering its every detail; mastery takes years, not one or two seasons. In the anaerobic system, strokes often break down; thus, age-group swimmers who frequent this system often develop poor strokes.

If the focus is on anaerobic training, age-group swimmers may be faster for a particular season, but they have taxed their bodies, which can cause them to burn out at a younger age or stagnate when they get older. They haven't trained at the aerobic level adequately; and they have developed poor training habits. They need to develop endurance—the ability to sustain the sport over time—and need to work on stroke efficiency over speed. According to Jonty Skinner, anaerobic work is dangerous for age-group swimmers, because "high levels of muscle acidosis could over time undermine the aerobic process and change the makeup of energy delivery during competition" (Oregon Coaches' Clinic).

When swimmers hit thirteen and have built years of an endurance training base that they have maintained, then they have the background to move into the higher-end training zones periodically, as their bodies can handle it. Thus, swimmers should be older, strong, efficient, and experienced before entering into anaerobic training. If anaerobic work is pre-planned and timed appropriately, the swimmer will develop from a position of strength and in a way that their growing bodies can handle.

While keeping the age of the swimmer in mind, coaches still want to vary workout pace and combine training zones within a workout and within a season. Swimming at one intensity can be stagnating. How much the pace changes depends not only on age, but also on the skill level of the swimmer, as well as the time of the season and the level of conditioning attained.

Heart rate

Young swimmers can learn to read their pulses. First, you need to teach them how to find the carotid artery (on the neck) with the two fingers that are next to the thumb. This may be difficult for them at first, so encourage them to move their fingers around until they can find it. If they are trying this for the first time, it helps to have them do this before and after a swim, so they can see the difference. Also, if they can't find it before the swim, they certainly will find it afterwards, and then will better understand what they are hunting for.

There are several ways you can teach the counting: hold for ten seconds, count beats, then multiply by six; hold for fifteen seconds, count beats, then multiply by four; hold for thirty seconds, count beats, then multiply by two. Holding for ten seconds is the most common method. A coach should choose one method and teach that method only; otherwise, swimmers become confused.

Also, explain why they are doing this. The pulse will indicate exercise intensity. Swimmers can monitor heart rate and know how hard they are working. If the coach asks swimmers to swim a set at 70% intensity (or, depending on the age and resting heart rate, a pulse of 27 X 6, or 162), swimmers know exactly what is expected of them; they know when they are swimming that set too hard or not hard enough. They know that it is not just a matter of swimming the distance, but it is also the quality of the swim. They will have a better understanding of the relationship between effort and improvement. If swimmers are swimming, and they aren't improving, they need to increase the effort put into the swims. And two swimmers can swim the same distance at the same speed and have different heart rates, depending on the ease of motion (stroke fluidity) and the level of conditioning. Thus, a coach cannot standardize a workout and have it work the same for all swimmers.

Once swimmers learn to read their pulses, this should be a regular part of their workout. They can incorporate this into the workout during the rests, and eventually they will do this without having to be reminded.

Those swimming to attain a level of fitness want to maintain a moderate pulse rate (50-75%) for at least twenty to forty minutes, three to five times per week (American Heart Association). This will lead a person to a healthier and happier life. Fitness is a valuable goal in itself.

Swimmers training for competition will shoot for an improved performance rather than an improved fitness goal. First, how much age-group swimmers practice per week depends on age and skill level. While eight-and-unders may practice four times a week, ten-and-unders may practice five. Advanced swimmers, especially over twelve, may practice eight times per week. Next, practice time can vary from one to two hours, depending again on age and skill level. In addition to the number of swims per week and the duration of each swim, the quality of the swim is important. Swimming at 65% effort is the low end of the training heart rate; 92% is the high end. Swimmers begin the season at the low end, and as they become conditioned, higher-intensity swims increase.

Heart rate methods

Method A: Take the maximum heart rate, which is 220, and subtract age to get an estimated max. Then subtract the resting heart rate (which will vary with each person) to get the heart-rate reserve. The heart-rate reserve represents the difference between the maximum heart rate and the swimmer's resting heart rate. Multiply by .60 to attain a fitness pace (60% of the difference between the resting and maximum heart rate) or .80 to attain an improved performance pace (80% of the difference between the resting and maximum heart rate). Add the resting rate to one of these totals, and this will tell a swimmer what the heart rate is when he or she is exerting 60% or 80% effort (American Red Cross).

For example, a fifteen-year-old's estimated max equals 205. Subtract his resting heart rate, which is 65; this equals 140 (his heart-rate reserve). Multiply by .80 (improved performance pace); this equals 112 (80% of the difference between the resting and maximum heart rate). Add the resting heart rate of 65 to get the final figure, a heart rate of 177 per minute.

This method is too complicated for most age-group swimmers.

Method B: The American Red Cross, as well as the American Heart Association, have charts that present averages per age and resting heart rate, so you get a rough rather than exact figure. This may be adequate for some age-group programs. Some coaches ask swimmers to memorize their numbers instead of doing all of this math at the side of the pool, which makes sense. The fifteen-year-old, trying to apply 80% effort, memorizes the number that is equivalent to that: 29.5 (which multiplied by 6 equals 177).

Method C: If a coach wants an exact, rather than a rough calculation per swimmer, this is going to take some time out of the pool, with swimmers and coaches working together. You can begin each season by asking swimmers to write down their ages and resting heart rates. The older swimmers will be able to do the math; the younger ones won't, and thus coaches or older swimmers can do it for them. Then, each swimmer will receive numbers (the heart rate divisible by six) for each training zone (A1, A2, etc.) and be asked to memorize them. These numbers can be written on a card and referred to if swimmer and coach forget. Then throughout the season, when swimmers are asked to swim a set at a particular (for example, A3) intensity, they will draw upon that number and use it as a guide. They can take their ten-second pulse at the poolside to check themselves; coaches can periodically write it down and do the math.

Stroke length versus stroke velocity

When stretching out a stroke, a swimmer gains efficiency. A longer stroke is a smoother stroke. This means less drag, and thus less energy expended per stroke. In the crawl and backstroke, a swimmer attains more stroke length (SL) if he or she rolls the body while stretching. Similarly, more stretch is attained in the breaststroke and butterfly if the body undulates. No matter the stroke, core movement maximizes stretch; and when swimming these strokes flat, a swimmer attains less stroke length.

During long, continuous swims, a swimmer will relax and in doing so, especially over time, will increase stroke length. An increase in stroke length will make a swimmer faster, even if he or she appears to be—and is—expending less energy. Long, continuous swims are isokinetic and thus increase overall strength. Factor in a focus on technique, so that swimmers hit the correct power points during the power phase. A strong swimmer will not reach maximum potential if he or she does not execute a stroke correctly. The stronger the swimmer, the greater the press and push during the power phase, the greater the distance per stroke (DPS). The stronger the swimmer, the greater potential for a more powerful power phase.

Stroke rate (SR) refers to the time it takes each arm to stroke. Cycle rate (CR) refers to the time it takes to complete one stroke cycle. To complete one cycle, the left and right arms alternate in the crawl while both arms move simultaneously in the butterfly and breaststroke. You can calculate seconds per stroke (SPS) and seconds per cycle (SPC).

Short, high-intensity swims (sprints) develop stroke rate. A swimmer practices swimming fast in order to be fast. After an adequate rest, the swimmer sprints again. To determine whether a rest is adequate or not, note whether the swimmer's stroke breaks down during a swim. If so, the rest was not adequate. Thus, the goal is to swim fast, but maintain good stroke technique. To sprint, a swimmer must be in good condition and have a high energy level. Sprints are integrated into every practice at the height of the season.

Stroke length and stroke rate can be calculated manually by counting the number of strokes it takes to swim a certain distance in a certain time. Swimmers should have a stroke count for each stroke. To figure out maximum stroke length in a particular stroke, a swimmer swims 25 yards at a moderate pace, at 60% of his or her heart rate. This gives the swimmer a baseline stroke count in that stroke, which he or she can then work on improving. Take the baseline stroke count, and while maintaining the pace, decrease by one stroke, then try for two less, then for three less. Thus, a swimmer stretches out his or her stroke to its maximum by subtracting one stroke per 25 yards and then another and then another, trying to gain as much distance per stroke as possible. Next, the swimmer tries to hold the maximum stroke length when increasing the pace of his or her swim to 70% of the heart rate. Then he or she shoots for 80% of the heart rate. At what pace does the swimmer lose maximum stroke length?

Swimmers want to achieve their fastest rate while stretching out as far as they can. But stroke length and stroke rate cannot co-exist at their maximums. As stroke rate increases, stroke length decreases and vice versa. Thus, swimmers need to find a balance between the two, which means they will inevitably have to lean one way or the other depending upon the event they are training for. A sprinter will lean toward rate while a distance swimmer will lean toward length.

Stroke-monitor watches are well worth the investment, but if they are not an option for your swimmers, remember it is always good for swimmers to know how to function on their own without technology. When establishing baselines for stroke length and rate per yardage, record the results in a notebook once a week. Over time, you can track exactly how fast you want swimmers to be turning their arms over, as well as how much they should be stretching their stroke per a particular event.

Interval training

Intervals are a series of repeat swims, with a controlled period of rest. They should be moderate-to-high intensity sets, with the rests designed to allow the athlete to recover enough to continue. They can be short (for example, lasting thirty minutes each) or can be long (for example, lasting two minutes each). Short intervals increase a swimmer's explosive power while long intervals help a swimmer tolerate lactic acid, as well as condition the body to eliminate lactic acid faster. The four variables in interval training are: 1) the number of swims; 2) the distance of each swim; 3) the speed of each swim; 4) the length of rest between swims.

Interval training improves a swimmer's endurance and speed. Intervals also add variety to a workout. For example, instead of swimming 500 yards , the swimmer swims 5 X 100 or 10 X 50, with a timed rest in-between. Hold the times for each repetition, or descend with each swim. Vary the interval at which a swimmer leaves—say 5 X 100 on 1:20/1:30/2:00—allowing more or less rest.

The type of interval training done depends on the swimmer's skill level, strength, endurance, and on the training objective. For example, if a swimmer is targeting a particular event at a particular meet, he or she will want to practice repeats of that distance.

Hypoxic training

This type of training is done when swimming short distances. Swimmers hold the breath or vary the breathing pattern to 1) work on long, smooth strokes; 2) see how little oxygen is needed when swimming long and smooth; 3) work on body position and core control and core movements; 4) increase heart rate; 5) build cardiovascular endurance; 6) increase lung capacity.

As a synchronized swimming coach, each season I watch young swimmers increase their lung power. They begin the program able to hold their breath for only so long. Their ability to execute a figure depends not only on coordination and skill, but also on breath control. As they push (over time) to stay under longer, because they want to accomplish that harder figure, their lung capacity increases. And as their level of conditioning increases, they can hold their breath for a longer time. In this case, as in the case of the swim teamer, conditioning is a long-term process that extends beyond one season.

When swim teamers "play around" with breath control, the result is that they become more aware of how much they are in control of their breath, rather than their breath being in control of them. The breath always fits into the roll or undulating of the stroke, but it can fit in every two, three, four, five, or more breaths. When losing oxygen, adaptations can be made in one's stroke to make it through a swim.

Distance versus over-distance training

When training age-group swimmers for distance events, focus on increasing their endurance through long, evenly paced swims and short rests. This falls right in line with their need to establish an aerobic base anyway. While each swim is evenly paced, a combination of aerobic intensities should be included in the workout, especially as the season progresses. The coach determines the training zone, and the swimmer sets the pace while stretching out his or her stroke and relaxing during recovery.

Over-distance training refers to a swimmer training for a specific event by swimming more than the distance of that event. For the 100-yard backstroke event, a swimmer trains with 125-yard sets. Over-distance training builds endurance, so that swimmers can more easily go the distance of the race plus more. It also builds confidence and makes competition for young swimmers less threatening. There is no question that they can make the distance, and they need to know that, when they dive in the water on competition day.

Crosstraining versus specificity training

Crosstraining refers to building strength and endurance for one sport by performing other sports. For example, jumping up steps will strengthen legs and could enhance a swimmer's performance. Running and bicycling will build endurance, but the question is to what degree does the participation in these activities affect a swimmer's performance? Is time spent running, better spent in the pool?

Specificity training refers to training for a specific activity by doing that activity. An athlete is not necessarily in shape for one sport, just because he or she is in shape for another. He or she cannot get into shape for swimming by running. In fact, some coaches believe that an athlete cannot mix two sports in the same season and be as efficient. When an athlete divides time and energy, he or she cannot give one-hundred percent to either sport. Specificity training also refers to targeting a particular event (such as the 100 meter butterfly) and training specifically for that event.

Heavy training versus overtraining

When athletes train at a high intensity for a particular length of time, they may or may not be overtraining, for two athletes handle the same training program differently. One swimmer may thrive on intense training while another falls apart and performs below potential when training too hard or too much. Actually, the one swimmer who thrives on intense training can also reach a point when training becomes too hard or too much; it's just that his or her threshold is higher than another's. Intense periods of training can be beneficial, as long as they are kept short (four to eight weeks, depending on the age of the swimmers) and as long as the athlete recovers adequately between workouts.

Symptoms of overtraining include chronic fatigue, loss of skill and strength, illness, injury, loss of motivation, mood disturbances, loss of appetite, weight loss, inability to sleep, dread of practice, and inevitably, decline in performance. First aid involves more rest and less work. It's better to stay away from practice altogether, until energy and enthusiasm resume, rather than to continue in this state.

Alternating hard/easy: Exercising hard every day is mentally, emotionally, and physically stressful. Most people will burn out under that kind of stress, and especially age-group swimmers. Thus, easy days should follow intense workouts. On easy days, athletes work out, but at a lower intensity.

Dry-land training

While the age and condition of the age-group swimmer is always a factor, as a rule dry-land training should focus on flexibility and on exercises that refine technique. An example of the latter: While lying on their backs on the deck, swimmers alternate between a tight tuck and a fully extended and well-executed streamline. Strength training for age-group swimmers should be done in the water, preceded by and followed with flexibility drills. Thus, they can develop strength without risking range of motion. Strength training should be carefully monitored, so age-group swimmers do not get injured.

Older, advanced age-group swimmers will be interested in building strength. Swimmers want to be strong, because stronger means faster. Building strength is also one way for swimmers to make the most of what they have. The stronger the muscles, the more they can control their bodies. Muscles are strengthened through three kinds of exercise: isokinetic, isometric, and isotonic.

For age-group swimmers isokinetic exercise—"lifting, pulling or pushing variable weight or resistance at a constant speed" (*Webster's* 1013)—is the most applicable. Swimming is in itself isokinetic. And the faster a swimmer moves through the water, the more resistance he or she encounters. When adding equipment, such as paddles, a swimmer adds further resistance, which increases muscle tension.

Isometric exercise "strengthens specific muscles...by pitting one muscle or part of the body against another or against an immovable object" (*Webster's* 1013). Example: pushing against a wall. Isotonic exercise shortens muscles while developing tension. This is done by "lifting a constant amount of weight at variable speeds through a range of motion" (*Webster's* 1014). Example: lifting weight.

While lifting weight is one way to develop strength, in an age-group swimming program, it would only apply to males who are in high school. Female, high-school swimmers should not touch weights; the risk of injury is too great. For high-school males, a weight trainer should closely monitor the activity, so that no one is injured. They do not want to work the arms and shoulders too much, because if they injure those, they can't swim. They can work the legs with less risk of injury, and this can be valuable, for a lot of races are won because of a strong kick.

Another important consideration when lifting weights: Swimmers do not want to bulk up too much, because 1) they will be less flexible, and that will have a negative affect on all their strokes; and 2) they will have to carry more weight through the water, which means they will have to apply more effort to their swims (than if they were lighter) to achieve the same result.

Training With Equipment

Training with equipment

Children usually like to work out with equipment. Equipment adds variety to swim practice; aids in learning skills; makes them stronger swimmers (by adding weight or resistance); and gives them a different feel for the water, or makes them more aware of how a stroke should feel.

Equipment is something a swimmer must learn to use. First, show swimmers how to handle the equipment and give them reasons as to why it must be handled this way. All equipment should be respected, since the property belongs to the pool or the team and costs money. A piece of equipment should not be treated like a toy or handled roughly. Next, emphasize safety. Muscle strains and pulls can result, if equipment is not used wisely. Swimmers need to consider two things: 1) choosing equipment that fits; 2) not overdoing it.

Choosing equipment: I bought large paddles, which were obviously too large for me, for after using them a few times I experienced a shoulder pain I had never experienced in all my years of swimming. I swam without the paddles for a week, and the pain went away. The following week I put on the paddles again, and the pain resurfaced, so I took them off for good and bought a smaller, lighter paddle, with which I had no problem.

Not overdoing it: When I first started using my monofin, I had so much fun, and it seemed so simple that I didn't realize how much I was doing until the end of the week, when my lower back started to ache. I stopped using the fin until I healed; then, I started slowly and increased frequency, intensity, and time gradually.

When first training with any piece of equipment, doing too much too soon is dangerous. Swimmers need to listen to their bodies, and they need to share any important information with you, so that together you can work through a problem and find the best solution for them at the time. This is critical for age-group swimmers, whose bodies are continually changing.

Kinds of equipment

• Kickboards are effective 1) when teaching and learning skills; 2) when whip kicking, for swimmers can practice the kick at its actual depth; 3) when placed vertically rather than horizontally in the water, so that the swimmer moves through the water with added resistance. Kickboards also have drawbacks, such as encouraging a flat, rather than side-to-side flutter kick. A swimmer flutter kicking with a board while in a prone position typically lifts his or her head. The feet drop below the surface, and the swimmer then arches his or her back to hold the feet up. This gives the youngster an incorrect feeling for the crawl.

• Pull buoys: At first the pull buoy will be tricky for young swimmers, as they try to balance themselves in the water with it. This takes practice, but is a challenge they can accomplish. This piece of equipment can teach children more about buoyancy. Add something to your body, and buoyancy changes.

• Ankle straps: A band wrapped around the ankles teaches children to keep their legs together in the butterfly, although it does not teach them to kick from the hips. You can also use ankle straps to keep children from kicking altogether. They work the arm pull, strengthening that one part, and then put the stroke together again and should notice improvement. With the pull buoy, the legs stay up when swimmers are not kicking; without the pull buoy, the legs drag. Swimmers will have to stretch their bodies, press their heads and chests down, and use their cores much more than they normally do. This is a valuable exercise.

• Paddles are used for two reasons: 1) to teach technique, and that includes giving swimmers a feel for a movement; 2) to build muscle. I've heard some coaches say that paddles don't build muscle, but I know first-hand that they do. I use paddles in my own training program, and use them to increase resistance and build muscle, so I can be stronger and more powerful in the water. But I rarely use paddles with age-group swimmers until they have reached thirteen years of age. If I do put them on younger swimmers, it is to teach some fine point or to give them a brief feel for something. For example, I may want them to feel the push of the paddle against the water; then I want them to take the paddles off and feel again. Swimmers need to be able to coordinate a movement adequately on their own first before adding weight or resistance to what they are doing. Also, the younger the swimmer, the more physically vulnerable he or she is to joint and muscle injury.

Paddles come in many sizes and shapes. Age-group swimmers should use small, light paddles. Then a coach should question swimmers regularly, making sure that their muscles feel good prior to putting paddles on and still feel good after taking them off. The next day, pay attention to who still feels good and who might be sore. If soreness develops, a swimmer needs to stop using the paddles immediately, and for as long as it takes for the soreness to subside.

• Aquafins can be used on either the arms or the legs. In the freestyle, the fins make the swimmer lift the elbow higher out of the water. When used on the legs, the only way you can kick is from the hip. Used on the arm or leg, the fins add resistance and thus build muscle.

• Fins and Zoomers: Fins correct flat-feet problems in the crawl and backstroke. If a young swimmer has a natural breaststroke kick that he or she is having trouble breaking out of when swimming the other strokes, putting fins on may work when repeated verbal instruction doesn't. Zoomers are shorter than fins and provide added resistance. They provide a swimmer with a good leg workout; the swimmer who wears them can build muscle. Zoomers make you practice at a faster pace and increase your heart rate.

• Monofins come in different lengths and develop a stronger, faster dolphin kick. Not only is the dolphin kick used in the butterfly; it is also used in freestyle and backstroke events, when starting and turning.

• Snorkels: Training with a snorkel builds cardiovascular endurance. In addition to that, when a swimmer breathes with a snorkel, he or she breathes differently. Using a snorkel throws off a swimmer's rhythm, for breathing sets the rhythm of a stroke. Now the swimmer is in unknown territory, feeling the same stroke, but in a different way. Eliminate one part and the other parts have to compensate; the significance of the one missing part is better understood when you have to operate without it.

Snorkel training allows a swimmer to work on body balance and alignment in the crawl and in the butterfly. In all strokes, the head is the anchor that holds the body in line. In the butterfly, a swimmer can eliminate the vertical movement that accompanies the lift and breath, and can work on keeping the head down and stretching out. In the crawl, the focus is the same: keep the head down and stretch the stroke out. While the swimmer continues to roll from side-to-side, he or she never rolls enough for the mouth to clear the water. This emphasizes rolling to make the stroke more efficient rather than rolling to catch a breath.

• The Hydro Hip: Wearing this belt with fins adds resistance when a swimmer's body rolls in the backstroke and crawl. Wearing this piece of equipment makes the swimmer thrust his or her hips with more force. The result is that once the equipment comes off, the swimmer continues to thrust his or her hips with the same force, but without the added resistance, and will turn farther, with more ease.

• Foam balls of various sizes can be placed between the knees while swimmers are whip kicking on their front or back. This teaches swimmers to keep their knees inside their shoulders and to circle their lower legs around their knees.

• A bungee cord can be used in two ways: 1) to pull a swimmer in the same direction in which he or she is swimming; 2) to pull a swimmer in the opposite direction in which he or she is swimming. If you pull a swimmer in the same direction, he or she will have to swim fast to beat the cord. The purpose of this exercise is to increase speed. If you pull a swimmer in the opposite direction, he or she will have to pull hard to move forward. The purpose of this exercise is to increase resistance and develop strength.

• A stroke-monitor watch: This is a more accurate way (than counting) to determine stroke length and rate. It works well for older age-group swimmers who spend extra time in the water, swimming on their own. This allows them to monitor their swims and know they are reaching the quality they should. The watch—rather than a teammate or competitor in the next lane—pushes the swimmer. The watch also comes with a chronometer, so if swimmers are training in a pool without a pace clock, they can time not only their swims, but also their rests.

Considering Health

The benefits of exercise

Exercise is natural for the human body; inactivity is unnatural. Exercise is also necessary—for physical, mental, and emotional well-being.

The physical benefits of exercise are numerous. Exercise 1) strengthens the heart; 2) increases circulation by creating additional routes of blood supply to the heart and by enlarging arteries, making them less susceptible to clogging; 3) lowers the concentration of fat in the blood, thus lessening the chance of clogged arteries; 4) lowers fibrin levels in the blood, which may prevent blood clotting; 5) increases the amount of blood in the body, the number of red blood cells, and the hemoglobin in the blood, and thus oxygen is carried to the muscles and tissues more efficiently; 6) builds lung endurance (through heavy breathing and a large intake of oxygen); 7) lowers blood pressure; 8) helps fight off diseases, thus lowering the risk of heart disease, stroke, cancer, diabetes, and arthritis; 9) increases strength, flexibility, and coordination; 10) strengthens and elongates and tones the muscles; 11) strengthens bones and connecting tissue; 12) increases the metabolism; 13) decreases body fat and helps trim off excess weight; 14) increases aerobic and anaerobic capacity.

Exercise also stimulates the brain, makes a person more alert, increases his or her ability to concentrate, and improves memory. Exercise increases oxygen, which energizes not only the body, but also the mind. Exercise increases productivity and creativity.

Exercise increases self-esteem, reduces stress, and can relieve depression. Physical well-being leads to emotional well-being. Athletes are happier than sedentary people. Possible reasons: 1) Norepinephrine, "a brain chemical" that "carries messages between brain cells" increases with exercise; and "depressed people tend to have low levels of norepinephrine, while people who are in good moods have high levels" (Wagenvoord 14). 2) Exercise "increases the blood supply to the brain," which means the "brain receives more oxygen" (Mirkin and Hoffman 17). Wagonvoord says "evidence points to the fact that oxygen is an energizer for the mind and the body" (13). 3) Also, while athletes want to avoid a high-salt diet, for it can create feelings of lethargy and depression, they are less likely to have too much salt in their bodies, because exercise eliminates it.

Modern humankind, as a whole, is less active than their predecessors. As technology has increased, as our world has become more convenient, people have become less active. The human body was built for movement, not to sit at a desk and in front of a computer, not to sit on a couch watching television, and not to walk less while driving more. Thus, to compensate for a change in lifestyle, humankind more than ever has to seek out physical activity.

When children come to the pool and get that exercise, the immediate benefits are numerous, but so are the long-term. If children grow up feeling the benefits of physical activity, when they get older, there is a greater chance of them continuing to be physically active. An adult who has had a lifetime of physical activity knows what he or she is missing when without it.

The importance of proper nutrition

A coach needs to educate all swimmers, no matter their age, on proper nutrition and how it relates to their energy levels. While swimmers may already possess this knowledge from their parents, the coach needs to reinforce its importance. While you can't watch what your swimmers are eating when they are not at the pool, just talking about nutrition can make a difference to them. And while you can't be responsible for what they do before they come to practice or after they leave, you can use your influence to tell them the right way to eat.

Coaches play the role of nutritionist now, more than in prior generations, because more is known about the connection between eating and performing well; because good coaching has become more focused on details, and we are finding out that these details add up and make a difference; and because children today are not eating as well as other generations. More junk food is available, and children are not monitored as well, because parents are working more. Children, left unmonitored, often pick the wrong foods. This will effect their energy level, their behavior, and their outlook on life.

There is a direct link between eating and performing well. A swimmer won't have the energy to train at one-hundred percent if he or she doesn't eat the right foods. And if unable to apply full effort to the training process, a swimmer won't do his or her best on meet day. A coach would be negligent to leave out this necessary part of what it takes to be a great swimmer; and a serious swimmer will care about this and will want to strive to have the maximum amount of energy.

Parents needs to be involved in this educational process. Children learn from them more than from any other. Thus, meet with both the parents and the swimmers, and talk about the nutritional needs of athletes. Parents who were or still are athletes will understand this. You also may find parents who have an interest and background in nutrition.

Educating swimmers

A lot of information is available—in books, in magazines, or on the Internet—on what constitutes a proper diet. While experts often disagree, there are some common theories: 1) eat a variety of foods, from the four basic food groups; 2) eat plenty of fruits and vegetables; 3) balance fat, carbohydrates, and protein intake (but the percentages vary from expert to expert); 4) do not exceed 30% fat (especially watch the intake of saturated fat); 5) use sugar and salt in moderation; 6) do not skip breakfast; 7) drink a lot of water; 8) maintain a healthy weight.

We also need to look at the individual when determining the best diet. One of the biggest fallacies in the dieting world is that one diet is right for all people. At one point, my family owned a horse. I was amazed by how much expert horse people differed over what to feed a horse. I came up with a simple philosophy then, that can also apply to swimmers: Get to know your horse, or get to know your swimmer. When determining the right balance of foods per individual, you need to see how he or she responds to foods.

Consider working with a local nutritionist who has a background in youth sports. Ask the nutritionist to speak to the team twice a year—once in the beginning of short-course season and once in the beginning of long-course season. Because age-group swimmers aren't usually competing on an elite level, it's foolish for them to talk with a nutritionist on a regular basis.

The nutritionist who spoke to my team emphasized that growing children should eat a variety of foods from the four basic food groups: vegetables and fruits; meat, poultry, fish, and beans; dairy products; breads, cereals, and grains. The focus was on a well-balanced diet. Children were then educated on what foods fell into what categories, and then given an assignment. Swimmers kept a three-week journal, recording everything they ate and drank. They also recorded how much sleep they were getting and how much yardage they were doing. Thus, when a swimmer felt low, we could better analyze the reason.

After three weeks, we (coaches, swimmers, and parents) talked about "how it went." Everyone agreed that the experience was worthwhile. The swimmers commented that the journal made them more aware of what they were eating and helped them to differentiate between what was good and bad for them. They learned about the varieties of food needed to maintain a balance. The consensus was that it was easy to fall off the health track if they didn't make a conscious effort to eat the right balance of foods. The exercise also helped parents to be more aware of what their children were eating.

Keeping the journal was seen as an educational process, done to help, not hinder, the swimmer. Always keep the goal of the activity in mind: to help the swimmer to have the energy to perform at his or her highest level. We all agreed that keeping a daily record could get tedious, if it went beyond the three-week time frame.

Fluids

The human body requires at least six glasses of fluid a day. Athletes need more than that. Swimmers, like other athletes, sweat while working out, even though they are in the water. When a swimmer dehydrates, his or her cells can't built oxygen; can't utilize energy efficiently; and can't produce urine, and thus toxic products build up in the bloodstream.

Symptoms of dehydration: 1) fatigue; 2) light-headedness, 3) dark-colored urine; 4) nausea; 5) muscle cramps; 6) decrease in training performance. Ironically, thirst is not included. First aid: Drink plenty of fluids before, during, and after a workout. Pure water is best; juices are better than soft drinks. Soft drinks often contain caffeine and can be high in sugar.

While coffee drinking may not be an issue with age-group swimmers, soft drinks are also sources of caffeine, and swimmers should avoid caffeine. Caffeine 1)) is a diuretic and promotes dehydration; 2) raises the insulin level, which will lower the blood sugar level and make a swimmer tired; 3) tells the body to burn more fat and less carbohydrate. This may sound good, but glycogen, if not used, will convert into fat.

A poor diet

Junk food—whether we are talking about a little or a lot—is detrimental to a swimmer's energy. *A little* junk food in the diet means wasted calories—calories spent on junk rather than good food. Yet an athlete needs more good food than the average person, in fact depends on it to keep up with the increasing demands of a competitive season. To replace the daily nutritional requirements even minimally with junk means less energy. Thus, to eat *a lot* of junk food is a disaster.

Some swimmers may have a vague, rather than concrete, idea of what you mean by junk food; thus, talk to them about specific foods that are good and bad. Talk to them about what they are eating and what kind of foods they should eat to get the energy they need. For example, an apple or orange is better than a candy bar or a bag of chips.

Symptoms of a poor diet: 1) fatigue; 2) inability to work hard; 3) poor recovery from workouts; 4) frequent or lingering colds or other illnesses; 5) inability to concentrate; 6) lack of enthusiasm; 7) mood swings; 8) depression.

First aid: If a swimmer is fatigued often, talk to the parents. Together you might be able to figure out if diet is the source of the problem. If not, suggest that the child see a doctor.

Considering weight and body fat

Ideal weight will vary from one person to another. Height and bone structure need to be factored in. Then there is an ideal range that a small-, medium-, or large-boned person at X height can fall into. If a swimmer eats a healthy diet in combination with a regular training program, his or her body should naturally fall at its appropriate weight. When a swimmer trains hard, he or she gains muscle and loses body fat.

Some believe it is more important to focus on the body-fat-to-lean-muscle-mass ratio than on weight. An overweight swimmer wants to cut body fat, not by starving, but with a healthy diet. While fat helps a person float, having excess amounts of it means moving a larger body through the water, which in turn means more drag.

Many people swim at a fitness level and think that because they are active that a high-carbohydrate, low-fat diet applies to them. They then gain, rather than lose, weight and come to a consensus that swimming is not a weight-losing activity. Swimming is a weight-losing activity, but only if done at a competitive level, meaning over 4,000 yards six time per week. Also, in reading Barry Sears *Mastering The Zone*, we find out that "controlling the overall amount of carbohydrate in a meal is critical" (351). He advocates a "protein-adequate, carbohydrate-moderate, low-fat diet rich in fruits and vegetables," (307) and interestingly relates how several Olympic swimmers have benefited from this (304-306).

At age thirteen and fourteen, girls begin to fill out; they acquire hips, thighs, and bosoms. And I've frequently seen girls at this age slow down. There is no reason for this, if they keep the body-fat-to-lean-muscle-mass ratio in check. Girls can also slow down if they go on a starvation diet. I refer to girls, for as teenagers, they are more apt to diet than boys, and yet if they are athletes, they have to maintain a high energy level.

Do not let your swimmers starve themselves to be the ideal weight. This will not only affect their energy, but also their attitude. While a swimmer will perform at his or her highest if at an ideal weight, ideal weight needs to be achieved in a healthy way. Health is always the priority, and especially when working with growing children.

When to eat and when not to

A swimmer should eat in a relaxed, rather than rushed, manner at least one hour before working out. Thus, if the swimmer practices from 9-11 a.m., then breakfast should begin at 7:30 and be done by 8:00. The athlete who doesn't follow this rule 1) won't be able to push hard; 2) won't be able to move well; 3) will feel heavy; 4) may feel sick; 5) may get cramps.

I have heard swimmers say, "Oh, I eat all the time before working out, and it doesn't affect me." I have a hard time believing that they are working out to their full potential if they can say that. A swimmer may eat and be active in an average way, but can't jump full force into heavy activity without feeling some repercussions. Once a swimmer tries this, he or she will never do it again, if working hard is the goal. The swimmer will feel the meal surfacing the minute he or she starts exerting any energy beyond warm-up pace. And the workout is shot for that day—unless the swimmer can attend another workout later.

One common scenario: the young swimmer who works out after school. Being a growing child—meaning often hungry—this swimmer will want an after-school snack. A light snack—one piece of something nutritious, like a piece of fruit—thirty minutes before working out is okay. Hopefully, the swimmer will have at least a thirty minute break between school and practice. If the child does not have this kind of a break, eating a substantial breakfast and lunch becomes all important.

Injury and Illness

Swimming related injuries and their causes

Injuries that occur at a swimming pool vary in kind and degree. The most common injuries occur to the muscle (knee, back) or the joint (shoulder, finger). These are usually a result of improper technique, improper training, or an unsafe behavior. Symptoms of injury include muscle soreness, stiffness, tenderness, redness, and swelling.

Injuries can result from incorrect stroke execution and then adding yardage without fixing the problem. For example, if a swimmer swims the crawl or backstroke flat, rather than with a body roll, he or she may injure the shoulder. If a swimmer whip kicks incorrectly while swimming the breaststroke, he or she may pull a muscle. Some technique related injuries occur over time while others happen instantaneously. A swimmer can usually feel a shoulder injury coming on, for the soreness (which results from stressing the joint) accumulates with added yardage. The knee injury, related directly to incorrect stroke execution, may occur in an instant. A swimmer may turn the knee the wrong way and pull a muscle.

Injuries related to training occur during a workout: if swimmers do not warm up or cool down enough, or at all; if they do not stretch; if they jump too quickly from the warmup to a high intensity set; if they do not incorporate adequate rest between sets; or if they work out much longer and harder than they are use to. For example, one day a swimmer, with zoomers on, dolphin kicks fifty laps, alternating between front, back, and side. The problem is, the swimmer normally doesn't do any dolphin kicking and has jumped from nothing to a lot; this will put a strain the lower back muscles.

Injuries also occur during a season: if athletes are not in shape and try to do too much too soon; if they experience an unrealistic increase in their workload from one week to the next; if they do not develop the proper aerobic base before training anaerobically; if they overdo anaerobic training; or if they swim hard day after day and do not take a day off.

Over-training injuries can happen to any athlete whose workload increases, and they especially occur if the increase is unrealistic. If age-group swimmers are overtraining under a coach's supervision, then the coach is not monitoring them appropriately. Also, while the majority of swimmers on a team may be fine with an increase of some particular movement, some individuals may not. Thus, swimmers need to understand the importance of communicating with their coach when feeling muscles soreness or pain.

On a rare occasion, older age-group swimmers may be motivated to such a degree that they overtrain themselves. This can occur if they practice on their own in addition to what they do with their coach. Extra practice should not be discouraged, but coaches need to be made aware of what their swimmers are doing, so they can keep an eye on them.

Why would a swimmer choose to overtrain? He or she may be excited about a particular goal and want quick success. And when an athlete is determined, it's amazing what he or she can achieve. When training, the body and mind need to work together. As badly as the mind may want something, the body will determine how fast and how far a person can be pushed. Thus, swimmers must learn to listen to their bodies.

Injuries also occur because of an unsafe behavior. They are called accidents, because they are not intentional, but often you can examine the cause and find an injury that could have been prevented by simply being more aware of a possible hazard. Diving holds the most potential for serious injury. Diving injuries result from diving too deep; diving into shallow water; slipping on the block or pool edge; and not making sure "the coast is clear" and diving on top of someone. Young swimmers may backstroke fast into the wall and jam their fingers. Swimmers have also been known to jam their heads into the wall. While this can hurt, it is usually a minor injury. In both of these backstroke situations, stringing up the flags at every workout and making sure that swimmers know how to use them can help to prevent an injury.

Injuries can happen away from the pool; some may affect a swimmer's season. For example, if a child breaks an arm or leg, he or she will be out of the water for awhile. Most age-group swimmers can afford to miss a little time in the water, for they have many opportunities to swim in the future. It is more important to heal properly. Even if they return to practice out of shape, they can eventually catch up.

First aid for injuries

When an athlete is injured, the coach needs to refer him or her to a physician, for treatment and advice. The coach then needs to be informed of the result, so he or she can monitor the athlete's activity accordingly. A coach should not challenge a physician's advice or encourage an athlete to go against what has been prescribed. Athletes look up to coaches and if there is a discrepancy, may follow what the coach says. If the coach is wrong, he or she could be sued. The coach is trained in CPR and First Aid, but not advanced medicine; the physician is the expert, whether he or she is a swimmer or not.

Since the reversibility rate in swimming is high, when an athlete is injured he or she shouldn't stop working out completely, unless this is what the "doctor orders." The athlete can give the injured body part a rest, but continue to work the uninjured parts, so he or she won't lose conditioning. For example, a swimmer with a shoulder injury can still get into the pool and kick, and may be able to execute a one-arm crawl. A swimmer with a knee injury can still stroke, and may be able to flutter and dolphin kick.

Whether a swimmer should keep swimming with an injury depends on the degree of the injury; his or her age and skill level; the importance of the goal (for example, a dual meet versus a championship meet) and how long and hard the swimmer has been working toward it; and most importantly, what the physician says. If a swimmer breaks a finger, the physician may give the okay to keep training. While going to a meet this way is a bit of a handicap, it won't affect his or her performance drastically. Older swimmers training for a major meet wouldn't let a minor injury set them back.

If a swimmer has to take a complete break from working out due to an injury, he or she should do everything possible to expedite the healing process. This means plenty of rest; rest is essential to recovery. Without rest, an injury will continue, and even grow worse. The more severe the injury, the longer the healing time. Thus, the earlier an injury is acknowledged and treated, the better.

A coach should not allow a swimmer to return to practice 1) without a physician's release; 2) if he or she cannot move a body part and appears to be in need of physical therapy; 3) if he or she is still in pain; 4) if he or she is experiencing a headache, dizziness, memory loss, or a fever.

Once the injured body part has healed, once the doctor has given the okay to return to the pool, the swimmer needs to ease into the workout gradually. He or she should feel an increased range of motion without pain. If the athlete feels soreness or pain, he or she has pushed too far and needs to cut back immediately; otherwise, he or she risks injuring it again.

The Benefits of Massage

Massage benefits athletes by 1) preventing injuries; 2) treating injuries; 3) helping athletes to relax and recover, both physically and mentally, from the stress that results from hard swims and hard days. As an athlete moves through a season, the workload increases. The body is in a constant state of stress and then adaptation, as the athlete pushes to higher levels of conditioning. Massage can provide relief when muscles are tight and sore. Through rubbing, kneading, direct pressure, or friction, any lactic acid remaining in the muscles will be release. If athletes recover from one swim before the next one, the chances of an injury occurring are lessened.

Massage is often prescribed to those athletes who have been injured and who have gone through the initial healing process. Physical therapy, which often includes massage, is needed to help the body to fully recover. The more fully an athlete recovers, the less likely the chances are of a re-occurring injury.

Illness

When age-group swimmers are sick, they need to rest and get well, not come to the pool and continue to train. Pushing the body when it is down makes matters worse and lengthens recovery. Also, when they do return, make sure that they build their bodies back up gradually rather than trying to do too much too soon. Some de-conditioning has taken place, and swimmers need to work from their point of capacity rather than from where they were prior to the illness.

Coaches should be aware that overtraining can cause illness. Pushing too hard is counter-productive, if in the long run it sets a swimmer back. A coach is responsible for both the health and safety of the swimmers. Some illnesses come on suddenly, and when they do, I recommend following the steps the American Red Cross lays out: check, call, care; follow your facility's Emergency Action Plan.

Rest (case study #30)

Many age-group swimmers work out for five days and take two days off. Swimmers need to take at least one day off per week. If they don't, they will burn out. Rest can also mean a good night's sleep, which will have a big impact on the workout the next day.

Tyler and Marcus, two eight-and-unders, usually attend practice full of energy and ready to work hard. One day they come to practice tired, and revert back to the poor crawl breathing habits that they had changed several workouts ago. They stop to rest much more often than usual. The coach notices the difference in their performance and ask them what is wrong. They tell him that they spent the night together and hardly slept.

When a swimmer attends a workout tired, two things can happen: He or she may or may not regain energy once in the water. It's counterproductive to push swimmers when they are feeling low. The only solution is to ease up on the swimmers, allow them to go home early; tell them to rest and return tomorrow refreshed. A coach should be concerned if this occurs often, but not if it happens once.

Swimmer's ear

Swimmer's ear results when water gets trapped in the ear and causes an irritation, maybe even an infection. If there is an accumulation of wax in a person's ear, this may cause water to get trapped there easily. In this case, a doctor can clean the wax out and solve the problem. Sometimes, swimmers do not clear water out of their ears after practice. They may be in a rush to get home; they may have a ride waiting for them. Swimmer's ear often, but not always, affects those swimmers who are in the water a lot. The greater the exposure, the greater the risk. But I have seen children in swimming lessons, who are not in the water as much as swim teamers, experience swimmer's ear, too.

Focus on prevention. Swimmers should wear caps when in the water. When practice is over, they should gently shake the water from their ears. Leaning the head to one side and pulling on the earlobe also helps the water to drain. Finally, they should dry their ears thoroughly with a towel.

Swimmer's ear is a condition that a swimmer can feel coming on. Symptoms include itching and pain. The sooner treatment begins, the less practice time the swimmer loses. Treatment: Once a twinge of swimmer's ear appears, dry out the ear with drops of 1/2 vinegar and 1/2 alcohol. Take a day off to give the ear a break; use this as a rest and recovery day. When the returning to the pool, wear earplugs and pull the cap over the ears.

If the earache becomes severe, or if a swimmer cannot get rid of it on his or her own, it's time to go to a physician. Ear drops, applied at night before bed, will bring instant relief. The swimmer follows the physician's advice, which unfortunately may mean staying out of the water for X number of days. But remember, age-group swimmers have the rest of their lives to swim. Not treating the problem appropriately will be detrimental to their health in the long run. Thus, do not stop treating the problem until it is corrected, and once it is corrected and the child returns to practice, monitor the ear.

Training the Mind

Psychological readiness

Athletes will be ready for competition and increasing levels of competition at varying rates. A coach needs to assess how a swimmer feels about competition prior to taking him or her to a first meet. A first meet should be on a novice level, with little pressure. The focus should be on doing one's best and having fun. The goals should be to establish a baseline; then in future meets, a swimmer can work on improvement.

Why compete? Competition 1) is challenging and motivating; 2) provides an athlete with a goal; 3) gives purpose to training; 4) is a way to test oneself; 5) and is—with the right attitude—fun. Why would an athlete not want to compete in a sport in which he or she is participating? Fear is the primary reason: fear of the unknown; fear of failure; fear of being in the limelight; or fear of parent, coach, or peer disapproval.

New swimmers should be encouraged and supported—by coaches, parents, and peers. A coach can do a lot to create an atmosphere of team spirit and goodwill, where experienced and rookie swimmers come together as one family. Make sure a swimmer has the skills to compete. If not, shoot for a future meet. Do not force a hesitant swimmer into competition; instead, win him or her over gradually. First ask the swimmer to watch a meet; then suggest trying one event, and build from there.

As age-group swimmers improve, they confront higher levels of competition and experience higher levels of stress. Thus, as they improve physically, they need to become mentally tougher. In readying an athlete for competition, a coach needs to analyze his or her emotional personality. Athletes vary in what they feel and how deeply they feel it. Two athletes may experience the same meet, may even share the same event and heat. One athlete may have a positive experience while the other athlete may have a negative one. With some athletes, an emotion passes quickly; for others, the feeling may linger.

A positive competitive experience

We can assume that the athlete who has a positive experience was, and still is, psychologically ready to compete. Thus, we need to turn our attention to those who attend a meet and have a negative experience. Your goal is for the swimmer to have a positive competitive experience. This leads to a better performance, which is positively reinforcing, and it usually leads to continued participation, which in turn leads to improvement. Thus, if a child has negative thoughts about competition, you want to change that.

There are two kinds of anxieties: cognitive and somatic. Cognitive anxieties occur within a person's head. Examples include negative thoughts, worries, self-doubt, being critical, disassociation, thinking of too many things, and the inability to concentrate. Somatic anxieties physically affect a person. Examples: butterflies in the stomach, cold hands, headaches, muscle spasms, hyperventilation, yawning, a fast heart rate, and the need to go to the bathroom.

Begin first aid by collaborating with the child on a list of positives and negatives. Then, resolve what you can; talk about what can't be changed. Coach and athlete can eliminate anxiety by considering "uncontrollables" (Goldburg). A swimmer can't control the outcome of a race, but can train hard and do his or her best. A swimmer can't control an opponent, but can be in control himself. He or she can't control the expectations of family, friends, or coach, but can prepare himself to make the best of whatever the outcome may be. He or she can't control anything about the meet: the heat or lane; the starter or the timers; or the water or air temperature. But a swimmer can control his or her expectations that these external factors be any different from what they are.

Often, just sharing anxieties will bring relief. Talk about all the things that can go wrong in a meet. What do we do if we lose our goggles; start out too fast or too slow; miss a turn; touch the pad, but not hard enough to stop the clock; flip our heels on deck; hit our head, hand, arm on wall; run into the lane line; miscount laps; forget which stroke comes next; or develop a cramp?

Swimmers must practice being comfortable with the uncomfortable. In practice, children can get hooked on swimming in a certain lane, on starting first instead of second, or on swimming a stroke technique set after every warmup. Suddenly, the coach follows the warmup with turns, and swimmers are distracted and asking why. A coach needs to create situations in practice that interrupt habit, so that children get use to having to swim under unusual circumstances. This will in turn ready them for competition, for competition in itself is the unusual, rather than usual circumstance.

Age-group swimmers must choose to feel positive in order to have a positive competitive experience. They need to focus on improvement rather than on winning. They have a lot to learn, and during the learning process should not expect too much of themselves. Competition should be seen as part of the learning experience. They need to have realistic rather than unrealistic expectations. Setting one's hopes too high can lead to nervousness, which can have a negative effect on performance.

Nerves

Most swimmers, no matter how experienced, have butterflies prior to competition. In fact, it would be odd if a swimmer did not get nervous to some degree prior to his or her event. But there is good and bad nervousness. Bad nervousness can rob a swimmer of the energy he or she needs. The race begins, and the swimmer is exhausted. Other effects include: tight muscles, restricted breathing (oxygen depletion setting in more quickly), a slow start, and sloppy mechanics (shorter strokes).

If a swimmer has applied one-hundred-percent effort to a good training program, he or she has less to feel nervous about. If the swimmer is not physically ready, he or she won't be psychologically ready. During a meet, I have heard excuses (often) as to what could have been done differently yesterday to perform better today. On meet day, it is too late for a swimmer to

think about all he or she could have done, or how hard he or she could have trained. The lesson can be gleamed from the present and used in the future.

Nervousness results when a swimmer focuses improperly. For example, the opponent is an uncontrollable, and focusing on any uncontrollable can cause tension. This particular uncontrollable is one I am susceptible to when competing. While waiting those last minutes before an event, I cannot make eye contact with the opponent. I have to focus on my block and my lane, as though I have tunnel vision. The other lanes and swimmers are out of sight and out of mind. I can visualize myself swimming in one lane in the pool, but cannot see the other swimmers in the other lanes. Nor can I focus on them once the race begins.

Just waiting for an event can be nerve-racking. Swimmers need to relax, stay loose, and maintain a good body temperature. Being too hot can drain a swimmer's energy; being too cold can cause stiffness and cramps. Swimmers need to stay busy, without utilizing energy needed for the race. Waiting around, being inactive, is not natural for youngsters. Swimmers can 1) walk around; 2) stretch; 3) watch others swim and root for them; 4) talk to or play games (such as cards) with teammates. For some swimmers, getting into the warm-up pool prior to their event for an easy, brief swim will lower tension without depleting energy; in fact, the experience may be energizing.

If a swimmer wants to perform at his or her best, it's important to develop strategies to stay calm. And with competitive experience, a swimmer is better able to deal with the tension.

Relaxation techniques

Relaxation techniques are an important part of both physical and mental training, and swimmers can apply them during practice, as well as during a meet. A swimmer enjoys practice more if he or she is relaxed. Relaxation is built into the recovery of each stroke. Relaxation is incorporated into the workout when the swimmer stops at the wall to rest for X minutes. Some sets are hard; some sets are easy. During a week, a coach balances hard days with easy days, because continual hard work leads to physical and mental burnout.

Anxieties related to coming to practice will affect a swimmer's ability to perform. He or she will be less motivated, less willing to apply full effort. If a swimmer attends practice tired, in a bad mood, not wanting to be there, he or she looks at each lap with an unwillingness. The more attached the swimmer becomes to these negative thoughts, the harder the laps become. How can the body truly *be there* if the mind is not?

Relaxation techniques during practice:

• *Chi Qung* exercises can be included into the warm-up or cool-down part of the workout. The idea is to combine deep breathing with slow, loose movement for the purpose of relaxing, centering oneself, clearing the mind, relieving stress, and acquiring energy. As the limbs move away from the body, the swimmer exhales (old or bad *chi*); when moving the limbs towards the body, he or she inhales (fresh or good *chi*). Fresh *chi* energized the body and the mind.

• Counting is an obvious meditation technique. The coach says, "Swim twenty laps," and the swimmer counts as he or she swims: one..., two..., three..., and so on. If counting yards rather than laps, then the meditation becomes 25..., 50..., 75..., and so on. A young swimmer gets so used to counting that once he or she becomes an adult, it's hard to swim without counting. Counting does block thoughts from entering the brain and taking over. If you let the mind wander, you lose count. Counting centers you back on what you are doing, which is swimming that lap.

• To break this habit, a swimmer can swim for X minutes without stopping, thus focusing on time rather than distance. A coach should give swimmers a chance to swim some of the workout without counting. Breaking a habit every once in awhile can rejuvenate the spirit.

• When you want swimmers to simply swim and relax while doing so, ask them to isolate and meditate on one of the five senses. For example, ask them to look for light, color, or shapes in the water; or ask them to listen to the many sounds within and around them as they swim.

Relaxation during a meet:

• Meditation is a relaxation technique. The swimmer focuses on the breath and travels inward, away from stressful surroundings. Experiencing the breaths with the senses blocks new thoughts from entering; thus, eventually the stream of consciousness slows. It's as though the mind has moved out of the rapids into calm water. When the mind is quiet, an athlete can put the activity he or she is performing into perspective.

The very nature of life is transient, and that temporariness can be placed into the competitive moment. A swimming meet is a series of moments that pass, no more or less important than any other time. A swimmer spends more time practicing for a meet than participating in it. Thus, it seems logical that the practice that goes into the meet is just as important as the meet itself.

A meditation in action

A swimmer's brain waves can be divided into delta, the deep sleep state; theta, the creative state; alpha, the relaxed and daydreamy state; and beta, the analytical and problem-solving states. Theta, the creative state, is action-oriented. This state deals with "now," which is where a swimmer performs best.

Swimming can be, with the right mind-set, a meditation in action. The swimmer is the artist; swimming is the art. The meditative swimmer strokes with mindfulness, or with full attention. If he or she is thinking of ten other things, he or she isn't fully experiencing the time or the place, and isn't fully experiencing life. The mind, in focusing on the activity, becomes one with it.

The whole world is a swimming pool, a body of water embedded in concrete that is going nowhere. We exist within the water (and air) around us. "Be here now," with all five senses. Become one with motion, and one with the water; become the water. Hear the rhythm of the breath and the rhythm of the stroke repeating itself through the water.

Visualization

Alpha, a relaxed and daydreamy state, can help a swimmer during practice. The swimmer visualizes himself or herself in the future, at the meet, swimming hard, and then climbing out of the pool with a smile, as though pleased with the race. This visualization seems real, as though it actually happened or will. Wanting to go there, thinking the experience will be positive, motivates the swimmer. Once there, the swimmer makes it positive because he or she has built the mind up for this.

Visualization can also help a swimmer during a meet. If a swimmer is nervous, he or she can daydream and travel out of his or her body. Prior to an event, a swimmer can close his or her eyes, breathe deeply, and visualize being in a positive place. For example, he or she can imagine standing on a particular beach. When returning to reality, the swimmer is calmer and has a better perspective. The swimmer is not trapped in the stressful situation, for he or she has chosen to "be here now" rather than on that beach.

The flow state

Energy flows harmoniously throughout the universe, and a swimmer is part of that, if he or she moves with this flow rather than against it. Energy flows in and out of the body as it changes place and form. We can gather and disperse energy, but cannot create or destroy it. Food, water, rest, and the environment (the wind or rain) energize the body. By quieting the mind, the body also gathers energy.

We need energy to sustain movement. A swimmer strokes, and energy flows from him or her into the water. The arm circles, creating the same pattern, on the same path repetitively and rhythmically. Energy moves from recovery to power phase, and from power phase to recovery.

The flow-state occurs in swimming when a swimmer applies as much physical and mental energy to his or her training as possible. Physically, he or she has pushed the limits; mentally, he or she has concentrated one-hundred percent on technique and training principles, and has applied the right effort in a forward direction, over time. At a certain point, all of the energy applied in that direction will carry the swimmer forward with little effort. It's as though the swimming is happening by itself, and the swimmer is just there.

The flow-state is the peak of all of a swimmer's hard work. It is the reward for those who apply themselves. This state can last from six to twenty-four hours; thus, a swimmer needs to catch it while he or she can. Ideally, he or she seeks to recreate the flow at each meet.

After the meet

After a meet, coach and swimmer should set aside time for self-assessment. Determine what went well and what needs to be improved. If a swimmer knows his or her limits, he can better focus on his or her possibilities. From there, the swimmer can continue to strive and improve.

Disappointments and defeats should be seen as learning experiences. The small goal is to cut an old time. Whether chipping away at a time or experiencing a major breakthrough, competitions are stepping-stones. Becoming "the best you can be" is a lifelong process and can only be determined if a swimmer gives one-hundred percent.

Good and bad days

Some days in the water are better than others. If a swimmer's energy is low, he or she knows it before getting into the water. Often, once in the water, he or she feels better.

On a bad day, a swimmer should still operate within the lower range of his or her potential. A swimmer should know the highs and lows of his or her potential and expect no more or less. If he or she has a bad day, there are other practices and other meets. On a bad day the swimmer still knows of what he or she is capable.

I have also seen swimmers who perform their best on the day of the meet, at a much higher level than what you had assessed as their potential. They thrive in the competitive situation and find it motivating, more so than practice. Something about that day, that moment pushes them to reach beyond their current limitations. For them, every meet day is a good day.

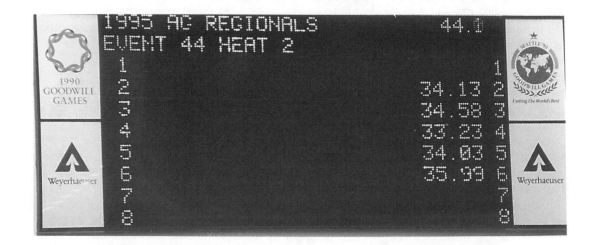

Competition

Types of meet leagues

Age-group swimmers and coaches may be involved in a year-round or seasonal program. There are city teams, county teams, YMCA teams, and private swim-club teams. Some teams compete primarily in USA Swimming sponsored meets, others compete primarily in local leagues, and others participate in both.

In order to swim in USA Swimming meets, a swimmer must be a registered member. This means annually completing a form and paying a registration fee. In USA Swimming meets, team members are split according to ability. Various time standards result in different meet categories: A, AA, AAA, etc. As a swimmer pares his time, he or she can move into a different category, which means attending a meet designed for that ability level.

Time standards encourage and motivate the age-group swimmer. They encourage those who are on the bottom now, but may be on the top someday. Even if they are not on the top someday, at least they have a chance to compete with swimmers who have similar times. Every swimmer, no matter his or her age or ability, is able to have a positive competitive experience. Swimmers know how their times stack up within their age group and know the times that need to be broken to move up, to the next level. As swimmers strive for the next level, they focus on their development rather than on winning.

Small versus large meets

Small meets 1) are stepping-stones for improvement; 2) provide a time and place for swimmer and coach to experiment with techniques and racing strategies, try new events, and then fine tune; 3) help swimmer and coach gauge whether they are on the right track when training; 4) prepare a swimmer for more intense competition and are necessary pre-championship experiences; 5) allow a swimmer to learn and improve in a low-pressure setting. A dual meet, one type of small meet, allows age-group swimmers to compete as a team rather than individually.

Championship meets are the large goal that swimmers work hardest to attain. In a large meet, a swimmer should not experiment with new techniques, race strategies, or events. The swimmer should enter the events he or she feels comfortable swimming and should have a race plan. He or she should be in peak condition.

A self-improvement meet

A self-improvement meet simulates an actual meet and can be held early in a season to give swimmers a baseline time. A swimmer competes against the clock, not against an opponent and not for a place or an award. Swimmers are encouraged to try events they haven't tried before. Relay teams can be established. Those who have never competed can prepare for the future; the unknown can create anxiety. This gives all swimmers additional experience; and the more experience, the less tense swimmers will be. Parents learn, too, and are ready for home meets.

Goals for this type of meet include 1) improving on a previous time; 2) providing a safe, tension-free place for swimmers and coaches to experiment with new techniques and race strategies; 3) readying swimmers for the real thing; 4) motivating swimmers with positive reinforcement (how they have improved); 5) allowing everyone a chance to participate and to participate together and give each other support; 6) teaching meet rules.

Meet organization

Swim meets are organized according to events, heats per event, age group, and gender. At most meets, a coach must submit swimmers' previous times, so that they can be seeded in a heat with swimmers of like times. Swimmers with the faster entry times are seeded in Lane #3 and Lane #4. The second fastest swimmers swim in Lane #5 and Lane #2.

Swimmers in the outer lanes are seeded against faster swimmers and are often affected by wave drag. But lane assignment minimally affects a race and is "an uncontrollable" (Goldburg) anyway. While swimming in a fast heat may discourage a young swimmer, it will also push him or her to better times. Swimming in a slow heat may be good for the ego, but can also give a swimmer a false sense of reality.

Jobs for parents

Depending on the meet, parents of swimmers may perform the following jobs:

• The meet coordinator assigns jobs to workers, coordinates their activities, and makes sure they have all the necessary supplies and information to do the job properly.

• The clerk-of-course seats swimmers according to their heat and lane, just prior to the race, and keeps the heats moving to the starting blocks.

• The referee supervises all workers and swimmers and keeps the meet running smoothly.

• Judges make sure that strokes, turns, and finishes are executed correctly. Lane judges determine the order in which contestants finish. A finish judge determines who places first, second, and third.

• The announcer 1) announces upcoming events and asks swimmers in those events to report to the clerk-of-course; 2) announces the names of the swimmers stepping onto the block; 3) announces results.

• The starter starts each heat of swimmers. "Swimmers, take your mark."

• Timers time a swimmer's race. Depending on the type of meet, there are two to three timers per lane.

• The runner runs the times from the timers to the office workers.

• The office workers perform a variety of jobs before, during, and after a meet. The jobs include: typing heat sheets, making copies, obtaining office supplies, ordering awards, recording results, tallying team points, distributing ribbons, typing the final results, and mailing them to other coaches.

• The lifeguard supervises the pool area.

• Marshalls oversee the spectator area and the two locker rooms.

Educating your swimmers

If swimmers are going to be competing, a coach has a lot more to teach them than how to work out. Besides refining technique, they need to learn the rules and strategies of competition.

The rules for competition can be found in the USA Swimming rulebook, which is distributed and printed annually. A broken rule results in disqualification. Examples of common DQs: a one-handed touch in the butterfly or breaststroke; a poorly executed breaststroke kick; flutter kicking off the wall in the butterfly and breaststroke events; missing the wall when flip turning; a second false start.

Teach the rules of competition by making them a regular part of practice. If swimmers practice correctly, there's a better chance they will perform correctly in a meet. For example, tell the swimmer about a single-hand touch in the fly or breast, and then make sure he or she makes the correction. If the swimmer repeats the mistake, repeat the lesson until it is learned. If more than one swimmer is struggling with the concept, isolate the skill, break it down, or think of some fun and interesting activity to get the point across.

Often, it takes repetition and practice before what you say sinks in. Some swimmers won't learn until they get disqualified, no matter how much you tell them a rule. Getting a DQ is a disappointing experience, and a coach wants to protect his or her swimmers from that disappointment. As a coach, though, you do everything you can, and the rest is up to the swimmer. Some students learn quickly, and some need more time, but will learn. Being disqualified does not have to be a negative experience, if the swimmer learns. As the swimmer progresses, becomes experienced, he or she should know the rules and no longer be in the position of getting disqualified.

Race strategy

Developing a race strategy for a particular event varies from one individual to the next. There is no one, right way. Coach and swimmer need to test various possibilities before deciding on one approach. Race strategies also vary from one event to the next. The same swimmer will have different race strategies for the 50 free, 100 free, and 200 free.

When determining a winning strategy for a particular event, divide the race into parts: the start, early-race, mid-race, late-race, the finish. The greater the distance of the swim, the more strategy is needed. In practice, experiment by swimming certain parts of the race harder than others and see how this affects the time. But be prepared for something different to occur during competition. When factoring in the adrenaline rush, strategy needs to be tested rather than pre-determined, and the smaller meets are the testing ground. Then the swimmer needs numerous competitive experiences to determine the best strategy per event.

Experimentation provides a swimmer with an added challenge. At a meet, there is so much more to focus on than winning. How about, "What is the best way for me to swim the 200 IM?" The age-group swimmer is constantly in a state of fine-tuning. Intermediate age-group swimmers (swimmers ranging in age from nine to twelve) are ready for this experimentation, although as children grow and their bodies change, they should continue to stay focused on this concept. They also need the help of a coach, no matter what their age.

Possible race-strategies for the 200 IM: 1) Think of eight 25s; swim 25 hard, 25 medium x 4, except for the last lap, where the swimmer gives all that is left. 2) Think of eight 25s; swim 25 medium, 25 hard x 4. 3) Think of four 50s; swim 50 hard, 50 medium x 2, except for the last lap, where the swimmer gives all that is left. 4) Think of four 50s; swim 50 medium, 50 hard x 2. 5) Think of two 100s; swim 25 hard, 50 medium, 25 hard x 2.

If a swimmer has any energy left late in the race, he or she should "go for it." Some swimmers conserve energy for a burst at the end. Others find energy at the end they didn't know they had. Or if a swimmer for some reason is psyched out and holding back, when the end looms it might be easy to let go.

A coach needs to watch each race and know how his or her swimmers performed in each event they entered. A coach needs to know, without looking at a piece of paper, the times of all his or her swimmers. The coach also needs to know what went right and what could have gone better. A good coach has a sharp mind, a good memory, pays attention to detail, and is in tune with each individual swimmer.

Team rules while at a meet

When at a meet, whether home or away:

• A coach should choose a spot and call everyone together. Swimmers need to stay close to the team, especially as their event nears. The coach should be able to find each swimmer at any time. Encourage swimmers to bring cards and other games to stay busy. They can also watch the meet and cheer for each other. Older, experienced swimmers should help the newer, younger swimmers. Swimmers need to keep their eyes and ears open for their event.

• When a swimmer arrives at the pool on competition day, he or she needs to warm up, stretch out, loosen up, and get wet. A swimmer needs to *feel* the pool and get into a competitive mind set. Visiting swimmers need to try starts and turns in a new pool.

Some swimmers need more of a warmup than others. A long warm up will help lower the level of mental tension. But swimmers do not want to go fast and wear themselves out prior to an event. Generally, when a swimmer begins to feel good in a warmup that means it's time to quit.

• During a meet, a pool is often available for warming up and cooling down, which is fine. Before an event, or between events, swimmers need to stay loose and cool. Heat zaps their energy. Thus, climbing into the warm-up pool prior to an event may be good for some youngsters. A light swim can also get rid of the jitters. But children may play in this pool and wear themselves out, although sitting and waiting for an event can be equally tiring. Children are not a good judge of how much is too much; thus they need to be monitored.

A coach does not have time to supervise his or her swimmers in a warm-up pool during a meet. The coach is busy making sure that swimmers make it to the clerk-of-course and starting block. A coach should be able to watch the meet, so he or she can know how each swimmer's race went. Thus, before the meet begins, it is best if a coach sets rules on when a swimmer can go to the warm-up pool and how much time he or she can spend there.

• Swimmers need to be courteous to each other and to the opposing team. When the opposing team is meeting on your turf, it is especially important that all of the swimmers on your team

are courteous and hospitable. The opposing team should be treated the same as guests arriving at your house for dinner.

It is important that competitors share a good time. Competition should be fun and especially for age-group swimmers. Swimming against a friendly team is much more fun than swimming against a snobby team. Swimmers from opposing teams can meet at the clerk-of-course, talk about the race over their nervousness, and possibly become friends. They may meet again during the season, at another meet. Swimmers broaden their horizons this way. Swimming extends beyond the limits of one pool in one town.

Pre-meet preparation

On the day before a competition, swimmers need to relax and not exert themselves too much. If they swim, they need an easy workout and stretch. They don't need to sprint or think about technique or race strategy. They should keep their mind off the meet, eat a good dinner, and go to bed early.

Pre-event meals should be light and should be scheduled three (and at least two) hours before warmup. Eating too much or too soon before swimming will slow a swimmer down and could cause stomach cramps. When an athlete eats, the heart pumps blood to the stomach; when an athlete exercises, the heart pumps blood to the muscles. If the blood is rushing to the stomach to aid digestion, the swimmer will have less for the muscles, and performance will be hindered.

Pre-event meals should not include sugar. Sugar makes the blood sugar rise, which causes the pancreas to produce insulin. Insulin draws sugar from the body, as does exercise. The result of trying to do both is low blood sugar, which makes the swimmer tired.

During a meet, I have seen children eat, and eat too much, simply because they are nervous, rather than hungry. Ask them to wait until after the meet; tell them eating will slow them down. Suggest they drink water. Swimmers need to drink a lot of fluid before, during, and after a competition, even if they do not feel thirsty. This will keep their energy up and their bodies cool and refreshed.

Case study #31

Sixteen-year-old Andrea cannot eat too early in the morning and warmups begin at 7:00 a.m. She eats a hearty dinner: pasta primavera, tossed salad, a roll, and a tall glass of milk. She goes to bed early, wakes, and drinks a glass of orange juice prior to climbing into the pool to warm up. She is out of the pool by 8:00 a.m., and the meet begins at 8:30. She isn't swimming for at least an hour into the meet. So, at this time, she eats a granola bar. She will drink water prior to swimming, but will not eat again until after the meet.

Scratching an event (case study #32)

Hilda was signed up for the 100 free, 100 back, and 200 IM. She felt so nervous about the 200 IM she was almost sick to her stomach; she was afraid she wouldn't make the distance, even though she had done this in practice many times. She wanted to scratch, but the coach convinced her not to. Despite her nervousness, she placed second and was glad (when the event was over) that she stayed in the race.

Once coach and swimmer have committed to an event, scratching is a letdown. Thus, for the swimmer's sake, there should be a legitimate reason. For example, if Hilda had gotten sick to her stomach, you would want to pull her out of the event. And once the decision to scratch has been made, there should be no regrets. A swimmer can make up for this in another event or meet.

Doping

FINA oversees all of the competitive aquatic sports and is thus the organization that is responsible for regulating those who need to be regulated. I would like to think that human beings are intelligent enough to act fairly in this world without having rules thrust upon them; that would make the world a better place for those who do play fair. Those who don't need rules to act ethically could live in a rule-free world. Unfortunately for the many, the few spoil the freedoms we could all have.

Doping is about the dishonesty of an individual, or a particular country that encourages its athletes to act unethically. This is a paradox; sports are supposed to teach values, such as acting with integrity. An athlete taking performance-enhancing drugs may think he is affecting only himself and those against whom he is racing. But this affects all young swimmers everywhere; this sends youngsters the wrong message.

It takes a certain person, low in morals, to cheat. This is done for status, image, to be in the limelight, or to fool others into believing he or she is a winner. This is done because the goal has become more important than the sport itself. But an athlete will never be able to feel like a winner if he or she has cheated; the athlete may be able to fool others, but cannot fool himself. To win dishonestly is to truly lose as a human being. This athlete will have to make amends with his or her consciousness.

To win honestly is the only meaningful way to win. All athletes must be on an equal footing in order for competition to be fair. Honesty and fairness is much more important than winning. This is the message that age-group swimmers need to hear.

APPENDIX

Works Consulted

American Heart Association. *Your Heart*. New York: Simon & Schuster Inc., 1995.

American National Red Cross. *CPR For The Professional Rescuer*. St. Louis: The American National Red Cross, 1993.

American National Red Cross. *Safety Training for Swim Coaches*. St. Louis: The American National Red Cross, 1988.

American National Red Cross. *Water Safety Instructor Manual*. St. Louis: The American National Red Cross, 1996.

Ames, Louise Bates, et al. *Your Ten to Fourteen Year Old*. New York: Dell Publishing, 1988.

Beard, Gertrude and Elizabeth Wood. *Massage Principles and Techniques*. Philadelphia: W.B. Saunders Company, 1964.

Berger, Melvin. *Sports Medicine*. New York: Thomas Y. Crowell, 1982.

Bunn, John W. *Scientific Principles of Coaching*. Englewood Cliffs: Prentice-Hall, Inc.,1955.

Cohen, Daniel. *Meditation*. New York: Dodd, Mean & Company, 1977.

Dudley, William, ed. *Sports in America*. San Diego: Greeenhaven Press, 1994.

Farber, Barry A. *Crisis in Education: Stress and Burnout in the American Teacher*. San Francisco: Jossey-Bass Publishers, 1991.

Gesell, Arnold, et al. *The Child from Five to Ten*. New York: Harper & Row, Publishers,1977.

Gesell, Arnold, et al. *Youth: The Years from Ten to Sixteen*. New York: Harper & Row, Publishers, 1956.

Ginott, Dr. Haim G. *Teacher & Child*. New York: Avon Books, 1972.

Goldburg, Alan. Oregon Coaches' Clinic. Sponsored by Oregon Swimming and USA Swimming. Seaside, Oregon. Fall 1997.

Goldstein, Robin. *"Stop Treating Me Like A Child"*. New York: Penguin Books, 1994.

Haas, Dr. Robert. *Eat To Win*. New York: New American Library, 1983.

Hyland, Drew A. *Philosophy of Sport*. New York: Paragon House, 1990.

Kaplan, Janice. *Women & Sports*. New York: The Viking Press, 1979.

Kauss, David R. *Peak Performance*. Englewood Cliffs: Prentice-Hall, Inc., 1980.

Leach, Penlope. *Children First*. New York: Alfred A. Knoft, Inc., 1994.

Macy, Sue. *Winning Ways*. New York: Henry Holt and Company, 1996.

Michener, James. *Sport in America*. Greenwich: Fawcett Crest, 1976.

Mirkin, Gabe and Marshall Hoffman, eds. *The sportsmedicine Book*. Boston: Little, Brown and Company, 1978.

Neal, Patsy E. and Thomas A Tutko. *Coaching Girls and Women*. Boston: Allyn and Bacon, 1975.

Orlick, Terry. *Psyching for Sport*. Champaign: Leisure Press, 1986.

Sears, Barry, Ph.D. *Enter The Zone*. New York: HarperCollins Publishers, 1995.

Sears, Barry, Ph.D. *Mastering The Zone*. New York: HarperCollins Publishers, 1997.

Silvia, Charles. *Lifesaving and Water Safety Today*. New York: Association Press, 1965.

Skinner, Jonty. Oregon Coaches' Clinic. Sponsored by Oregon Swimming and USA Swimming. Seaside, Oregon. Fall 1997.

Torrey, Lee. *Stretching the Limits*. New York: Dodd, Mead & Company, 1985.

Sports Training Manual for Synchronized Swimming. Indianapolis: United States Synchronized Swimming Sports Medicine Committee, 1992.

Wagenvoord, James. *The Swim Book*. Indianapolis: The BobbsMerrill Company, Inc., 1980.

Wagner, Tony. *How Schools Change*. Boston: Beacon Press, 1994.

Watkins, Robert, Bill Buhler and Patricia Loverock. *The Water Workout Recovery Program*. Chicago: Contemporary Books, Inc., 1988.

Webster's Encyclopedic Unabridged Dictionary of the English Language. 1996.

USA Swimming. *1999 Rules & Regulations*. Colorado Springs: USA Swimming, 1999.